Flavors of Emilia Romagna

Flavors of Italy

Rosalba Gioffrè
Gabriella Ganugi

Emilia Romagna

MᶜRae Books

ISBN 88-89272-03-1

This book was conceived, edited and designed by
McRae Books Srl, Borgo S. Croce 8, 50122, Florence, Italy
info@mcraebooks.com

Text: Rosalba Gioffrè and Gabriella Ganugi
Photography: Marco Lanza
Home Economist: Rosalba Gioffrè
Design: Marco Nardi
Layouts: Ornella Fassio, Adriano Nardi, Adina Stefania Dragomir, Sara Mathews
Translation from the Italian: First Edition
Editing: Alison Leach, Anne McRae, Helen Farrell

2 4 6 8 10 9 7 5 3

Color separations: Fotolito Toscana, Florence, Italy
Printed and bound in Italy by D'Auria Industrie Grafiche Spa

Contents

Introduction ▪ 7

Antipasti ▪ Appetizers 14

Primi Piatti ▪ First Courses 32

Secondi Piatti ▪ Main Courses 60

Verdure ▪ Vegetables 88

Dolci ▪ Desserts and Cookies 100

Index ▪ 118

Introduction

Although Emilia and Romagna are now united as one region and their inhabitants speak similar dialects, albeit with very dissimilar and distinct inflections, they have quite different histories and traditions. Emilia, which includes the landlocked plains of the provinces of Bologna, Modena, Reggio Emilia, Parma, and Piacenza, has been a rich and highly productive area since ancient times. The fertile Po River Valley has ensured that it has always been the region of Italy with the highest agricultural yields. The Emilians' way of life is an art, their speech soft and musical: Giuseppe Verdi and Arturo Toscanini both came from Emilia. People still use bicycles a great deal to get around; restaurants have artistic displays of local produce on show in their windows, and the gastronomy of the region reflects the soul of its people: rich and delicate, sumptuous and simple, rustic and full-blooded, yet refined.

Emilia produces enormous quantities of cured meats and cheese. This is the homeland of Parmesan cheese, known throughout the world, and also of the very best quality *prosciutto*—Parma ham. Emilia is also famous for its pasta dishes, of which *tortellini* is perhaps the best known. But there are many different kinds of pasta, usually egg-based and very often filled with meat, vegetable, herb, or ricotta cheese mixtures. Every town has its own specialty and villages just a few miles apart will have quite different traditions. Bologna is the hometown of one of the best known *ragù di carne* (meat sauces) which is served with all kinds of pasta.

Romagna, which lies along the Adriatic coast to the east of Emilia, includes the provinces of Ferrara, Ravenna, and Forlì. Until the nineteenth century, Romagna was one of the Papal States; in former times the Popes were renowned for being inflexible and tyrannical rulers and it is thus perfectly comprehensible that its inhabitants, who suffered

Although Emilia and Romagna now form one region, they were originally two states. They are separated by a river—the Rubicon—made famous by Julius Caesar's historic decision on January 11 in the year 49 to cross it and continue down to Rome, launching a tragic civil war. Caesar drove his rival Pompey out of the Italian peninsula and into Egypt, where the Roman dictator famously dallied with the Queen, Cleopatra.

Sunset in the fertile Po Valley.

For many Italians, the now prosperous coastal region with its tourist industry centered on the resorts of Rimini, Riccione, and Cattolica, evokes memories of simple, happy holidays, of *piadine* (flatbread) made with flour, water, salt, and lard and eaten with *squaquarone*, a soft local cheese which goes so well with these hot, freshly baked flatbreads. Filmmaker Federico Fellini was born in Rimini and he stayed faithful to his hometown throughout his life, adopting it as a sort of muse which inspired many of his movies. These paid tribute to the scents, aromas, food, and people of the town in a continual *Amarcord* (meaning "I remember" in the local dialect) of memories.

such poverty and hardship at their hands, should have become so violently anti-clerical, a trait still shared by some Romagnols.

The coastal strip of Romagna, bordering the Adriatic Sea, is known for its excellent seafood, which are used in a range of broiled (grilled) dishes and in soups and stews. One of the best and most typical dishes is the mixed grill of the fresh fish caught along the coast every morning.

Inland, the hilly province of Ferrara has a long and distinct tradition of its own, based around the medieval court. Veal, beef, chicken, and rabbit form the basis of most main courses in this province, which has always had a fairly large Jewish population. A particularly strong tradition of fruit growing in this area means that it supplies the whole of Europe with cherries, pears, apples, apricots, and other orchard fruits.

Differences in history, geography, and climate in Emilia Romagna, which stretches from the Tuscan-Emilian Appennine mountains in the south to the rich flatlands in the north and coastal plains to the east, have given rise to a gastronomic tradition with very varied tastes and ingredients, as rich and robust as it is elaborate and refined. Even so, there is much common ground. Both Emilians and Romagnols are wonderfully hearty eaters, exigent, and very proud of their local cuisines. They are convivial, and fond of eating and drinking while indulging in conversation and discussion. It is no surprise that Pellegrino Artusi (see pages 110–111), author of the first national cook book published after the unification of Italy, should have been born here.

Pork is a mainstay of local gastronomy. When a pig is butchered, virtually all the cuts are used, turned into sausages, prosciutto, pancetta, zamponi, various types of salami and cotechino, and many other types of cured meat. The pork fat, refined into lard, was the basic cooking fat for poor people in the past. It is still used for frying in Emilia Romagna.

Cured meats are typical of the entire region. Although Parma ham has acquired a worldwide reputation for its tenderness, color, and

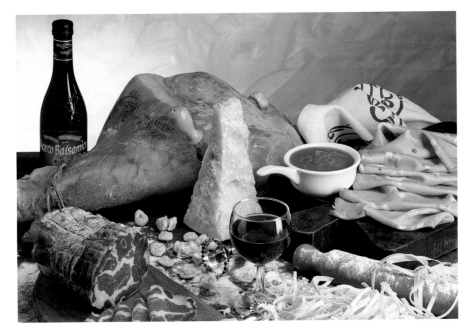

The cuisine of Emilia Romagna is largely based on cured meats, fresh pasta, and parmesan cheese. The local wines, both reds (such as Lambrusco and Gutturnio), and whites, are often *frizzante* (lightly sparkling). Initially puzzling for many, these wines go together superbly with the local foods.

taste, there are a host of other less well known types. Each city has its own specialty: Modena is famous for *zampone* (stuffed pig's foot/trotter) and *cotechino*, (large sausages that have been elevated from regional to national dishes) made with pork and pig's skin ground with pepper, garlic, salt, and spices. In Italy they are so highly regarded that they are now traditional for New Year's Eve dinner, served with lentils which, so legend has it, will bring good luck and prosperity for the year to come.

Ferrara is known for its *Salama da sugo*, which is made with various cuts of pork and flavored with wine and spices. *Salama* (as opposed to the more usual spelling of "*salame*") has long been regarded as an aphrodisiac and is served at wedding feasts to this day. *Salama* was hardly ever found outside Ferrara until the 1950s, when the writer Mario Soldati created the first TV series on Italian cooking. The program was a gastronomic journey through the regions of Italy, with particular emphasis on the Po Valley and Emilia Romagna. Soldati was thought to have

Mortadella comes from Bologna, where it has been made since about 1300. The name is derived from the Latin *mortarium*, the mortar in which the meat used to be pounded to a paste with spices. Its unmistakable scent pervades every *salumeria* (cured meats store).

ITALY

Emilia Romagna

ADRIATIC SEA

Piacenza

Parma

Ferrara

Reggio
nell'Emilia

Modena

BOLOGNA

Ravenna

Forli

Rimini

TYRRHENIAN SEA

exceeded the bounds of decency when he lifted a steaming hot *salama* from its pan and, sniffing it with relish, pronounced it perfect. *Salama* was completely unknown to most Italians at the time and when people read the newspapers the following day, they thought it was a typing error.

Fresh pasta is another of Emilia Romagna's culinary triumphs. The credit for inventing tortellini is still disputed between Emilia and Romagna, while the recipe, shapes, and stuffings of *cappelletti*, *ravioli*, and *anolini* vary from one household to another. It is impossible to identify a "standard" recipe. Each housewife prepares the filling and sheet of pasta dough in her own way, performing a sort of dance in front of her pastry board, automatically repeating the same gestures as her forebears without having to concentrate.

Other specialties such as *Crescenti* (see recipe, page 18), *Gnocco fritto*, and *Gnocco ingrassato* call for different types of pasta. These dishes have been part of the local peasant tradition for centuries. They provided a sustaining, high calorie midday meal for the country people who had to work hard in the fields from dawn to dusk and were not served as appetizers as they are today. *Gnocco fritto* is made with flour, salt, and water. Disk shaped and about ¼ in (5 mm) thick, it is fried in lard. *Gnocco ingrassato* is similar, although enriched by the addition of pieces of prosciutto and baked in the oven.

Parma, Reggio, and Piacenza all claim to be the birthplace of the most famous Italian cheese, authentic Parmesan. Mentioned by Boccaccio in his 14th century *Decameron*, it is now officially designated Parmigiano Reggiano to safeguard its quality and provenance.

Although less important than in other regions, some delicious desserts are served in Emilia Romagna. *Bensone* (see recipe, page 103) is a specialty of Modena and is still made to the same medieval recipe. *Sfrappole* (see recipe, page 105) are a Carnival treat. *Tortelli di Marmellata* (see recipe, page 104) with a sweet filling of jam, also date back to the Renaissance.

Bolognese tagliatelle should measure just under ½ in (8 mm) wide and ⅓ in (0.5 mm) thick when cooked. A special "confraternity" has been set up in Bologna to safeguard the standards of tortellini!

The cooking of this region reflects the mentality of its inhabitants and their belief in the magical properties of food. Eels from the Comacchio lagoons (below) cooked to Romagnol recipes have acquired a solemn and propitiatory role in the national culinary repertory when served as festive fare at Christmas time.

With the exception of Ferrara and Ravenna, all the provincial capitals of the region, with their buildings of white marble and mellow red brick, are linked by the Via Emilia. They are noted for their art, culture, gastronomy, and the friendliness of the people.

Europe's oldest university was founded in the regional capital of Bologna nine centuries ago. With its twin medieval towers soaring high above the city, it is still a center of learning, art, and music. Internationally, it is perhaps the city most closely identified with Italian food. *Tortellini in brodo* (see recipe, page 35), *Ragù alla bolognese* (Meat sauce, see recipe, page 40), mortadella, and *Fritto misto* are just some of its specialties.

Further north, Reggio Emilia is also a city of art, culture, and fine food. Theaters, palaces, and cathedrals abound in the city center. Local cooking is noted for its first courses, including *Cappelletti di magro Romagnoli* (see recipe, page 33), *Cappellacci di zucca* (see recipe, page 36), and *Lasagne*. Main courses include a variety of game and mushrooms from the Apennines, while the local Lambrusco wines add a special character all of their own.

Modena was once the splendid capital of the Dukes of Este. Its days of glory long gone, it is now a very prosperous, rather quiet provincial city, and the hometown of Ferrari cars. Apart from the almost inexhaustible variety of cured meats on sale in the local *salumerie*, Modena is the birthplace of balsamic vinegar which is now exported all over the world. The local Vignola cherries, fresh or preserved in alcohol, are also famous.

Pellegrino Artusi's hometown of Forlì has retained its medieval street plan and shares its gastronomic inheritance of fresh pasta, such as *tagliatelle*, *passatelli*, and *cappelletti*, with nearby Cesena, the birthplace of three popes.

The Este family once ruled the city of Ferrara, with its Romanesque cathedral with sculptures by Jacopo della Quercia. Local gastronomic delicacies, such as *Pasticcio alla ferrarese* (Maccheroni Pie

Ferrara-style), *Panpepato* (spice bread) and *Cappellacci di zucca* (see recipe, page 36), came from the court of the Dukes of Este. Specialties such as *Prosciutto d'oca* (cured goose meat) and *Buricco*, a type of large stuffed pasta with a chicken and rabbit filling instead of pork, are legacies of the city's formerly large Jewish community.

In proportion to its size, the province of Parma produces an impressively large number of quality foodstuffs: parmesan, *culatello*, prosciutto, wines, *anolini*, as well as *Tortelli di erbetta*, stuffed pasta traditionally served on the night of June 24 to celebrate the Feast of St. John.

The last stronghold of the Western Roman Empire, Ravenna is famous for the mosaics at San Vitalis, the Tomb of Galla Placidia, and the Baptistry of Sant'Apollinaris in classe. From the Pineta, a pine forest to the east of the city, come truffles and all sorts of herbs. The local specialty is the quaintly named *Frittatina agli uomini nudi* (fried naked men): they are actually little fishes.

Piacenza straddles the border between Emilia and Lombardy. The town hall, referred to as "il Gotico," is a masterpiece of 13th century Lombard architecture. Typical dishes include: dumplings made with flour, bread, and water, and served with a bean sauce and *Tortelli con le code*, a type of stuffed pasta, with a filling of ricotta and spinach. Mushrooms are plentiful and play an important part in the local cooking.

A lively seaside town, Rimini offers visitors entertainment, beaches, and architectural treasures such as the Malatesta Temple, the Arch of Augustus, and the Bridge of Tiberius. Its cooking is based mainly on fish, including *Brodetto dell'adriatico* (see recipe, page 62). First courses consist mainly of freshly made pasta and include *tagliatelle*, *maltagliati*, and *strozzapreti*.

The red brick Este Castle, complete with moat, is one of the most important surviving monuments from the medieval town of Ferrara.

The Adriatic coast is a haven for yachting and boating of all sorts. The port at Rimini is also the hub for the local fishing industry.

Antipasti

Flatbread	15
Fried vegetable pies	16
Savory pastry fritters	18
Fried mortadella	19
Rice and pumpkin pie	20
Savory pie	24
Salad with balsamic vinegar dressing	26
Parmesan cheese ice cream	27
Potato pie	29
Prosciutto with melon	30
Fritters in balsamic vinegar	31

Often consisting of fried pieces of unleavened dough, appetizers in Emilia Romagna can be hearty fare in which the traditions of centuries of peasant-style cooking remain vibrant. Drizzled with the local balsamic vinegar, many of these dishes are exquisite in their rustic simplicity. Aside from fritters, savory vegetable pies are a frequent alternative. These dishes also make nourishing light lunches. One of the most delicious and light appetizers comes from Parma, where the delicately flavored local ham is teamed with fresh cantaloupe, melon, or figs.

Piadina

Flatbread

Sift the flour, baking soda, and a generous dash of salt into a mixing bowl. Shape into a mound and make a well in the center. ▪ Pour in the lard and a little of the warm water. ▪ Gradually mix in the flour, adding a little more water, just sufficient to make a rather firm dough. ▪ Knead the dough on a work surface until smooth. Return to the bowl and cover with a cloth. Set aside for 30 minutes. ▪ Use a well-floured rolling pin and pastry board to roll out the dough into a very thin sheet (less than ⅛ in/2 mm thick). ▪ Cut out disks of 6–8 in/15–20 cm in diameter. Cook these on a griddle or dry-fry in a very hot cast iron skillet (frying pan), turning once. ▪ Serve very hot, with slices of prosciutto, salami, or cheese.

Serves: 6–8
Preparation: 25 minutes + 30 minutes' resting
Cooking: 15 minutes
Recipe grading: fairly easy

- 3⅓ cups/500 g unbleached all-purpose/strong, plain flour
- 1 teaspoon baking soda/ bicarbonate of soda
- dash of salt
- 4 tablespoons melted lard
- scant ½ cup/100 ml warm water

Suggested wine: a dry white (Trebbiano di Romagna)

This specialty from the Romagna region is a direct descendant of traditional unleavened flatbreads (or focaccias). It is a very old recipe, dating from before the introduction of yeast. These flatbreads are usually served with squaquarone, *a fresh white cheese closely resembling* stracchino *cheese. The traditional method of cooking was on a fireproof earthen-ware disk, heated on glowing embers until red hot.*

Serves: 6–8
Preparation: 30 minutes
Cooking: 20 minutes
Recipe grading: fairly easy

- 1¾ lb/800 g spinach, Swiss chard, or spinach beet
- 1 small onion, finely chopped
- 3 tablespoons butter
- salt and freshly ground black pepper
- 2⅔ cups/250 g all-purpose/plain flour
- 3 large eggs
- scant ½ cup/100 ml milk
- lard or olive or sunflower oil, for frying

Suggested wine: a dry or medium sparkling red (Lambrusco di Sorbara)

Cassoni

Fried vegetable pies

Wash the greens thoroughly and cook in a little salted, boiling water. ▪ Drain, then squeeze out the excess moisture and chop very coarsely. ▪ Fry the onion gently in the butter until it is pale golden brown. ▪ Add the spinach and fry briefly, stirring continuously. Season lightly with salt and pepper. ▪ Sift the flour and a dash of salt into a mixing bowl. Make a well in the center. ▪ Break the eggs into it and stir with a fork, gradually incorporating the flour and adding enough milk, a little at a time, to form a soft dough that leaves the sides of the bowl cleanly. ▪ Knead the dough until smooth. ▪ Using a well-floured rolling pin and board, roll the dough out into a thin sheet and cut out disks of 4 in/10 cm in diameter. ▪ Spread a little of the spinach filling over half of each disk (stopping well short of the edge). Fold the uncovered half over the top, to make semi-circular pies. ▪ Press down on the curved edges with the tines of a fork to seal tightly. ▪ Fry the pies until golden brown on both sides in plenty of very hot lard or oil. ▪ Drain on paper towels and serve while still very hot.

These are popular throughout Emilia Romagna with slight variations in the filling of spinach or other green leaf vegetables (wild or cultivated) depending on the locality. For a much simpler filling, fry the spinach briefly in a little oil. Season with salt and freshly ground pepper and add a small quantity of soaked, drained seedless white raisins (sultanas).

Serves: 8–10
Preparation: 40 minutes + 1 hour's resting
for the dough
Cooking: 20 minutes
Recipe grading: fairly easy

- 1½ oz/45 g compressed fresh yeast
  or 3 (¼ oz/7 g) packages active dry yeast
- 1 cup/250 ml warm water
- 3⅓ cups/500 g all-purpose/plain flour
- dash of salt
- 4 tablespoons melted lard
- oil or lard, for frying

Suggested wine: a dry, fruity white
(Albana di Romagna)

Crescenti

Savory pastry fritters

Dissolve the yeast in the warm water and set aside to rest for 15 minutes. ▪ Sift the flour and salt into a large bowl. Make a well in the center and pour in the lard and yeast mixture. Stir with a fork, gradually working in the flour, adding a little more water if needed. ▪ Transfer to a floured work surface and knead until the dough is smooth and elastic. ▪ Shape into a ball and leave to rise in the bowl, covered with a clean cloth, for about 1 hour. ▪ Roll out the dough into a sheet ⅛ in/3 mm thick. Cut into lozenges or rectangles about 2 in/5 cm long. ▪ Fry the fritters, a few at a time, in plenty of very hot oil or lard until golden brown all over. ▪ Drain on paper towels. ▪ Serve very hot.

An example of simple, tasty home cooking, this recipe is known all over Emilia under different names. They are known as Crescenti *in Bologna;* Gnocco fritto *in Reggio Emilia and Modena, and* Torta fritta *in Parma. They are always served very hot, either with very thin slices of prosciutto or other cured meats. For crisp, dry fritters, always use a small skillet (frying pan) and fry the fritters in small batches in plenty of oil.*

Mortadella fritta

Fried mortadella

Cut the mortadella slices into quarters and place in a bowl. Add sufficient warm milk to cover, then leave to stand for 2 hours. ▪ Drain and dry with paper towels and coat with flour. ▪ Lightly beat the egg and season with salt, pepper, and a dash of nutmeg. ▪ Dip the mortadella in the egg and then coat with the bread crumbs. ▪ Fry in plenty of very hot oil until golden brown. ▪ Drain on paper towels and serve very hot.

Serves: 6–8
Preparation: 15 minutes + 2 hours to soak the mortadella
Cooking: 10 minutes
Recipe grading: easy

- four ¼-in/5-mm thick slices of mortadella/Bologna sausage
- about 2 cups/500 ml warm milk
- ⅔ cup/100 g all-purpose/plain flour
- 1 large egg
- salt and freshly ground black pepper
- dash of nutmeg
- ¾ cup/90 g fine dry bread crumbs
- sunflower seed oil, for frying

Suggested wine: a dry or medium sparkling red (Lambrusco Grasparossa di Castelvetro)

In this recipe Bologna's famous mortadella or Bologna sausage, used throughout the region to flavor a variety of filling mixtures, and for croquettes and stuffed pasta fillings, becomes a star in its own right.

19

Serves: 6–8
Preparation: 30 minutes
Cooking: 45 minutes
Recipe grading: fairly easy

- 2 cups/500 ml water
- 1²⁄₃ cups/400 ml milk
- salt and freshly ground black pepper
- 1½ cups/300 g uncooked Italian rice
- piece of pumpkin weighing about 1 lb/500 g
- ½ cup/60 g freshly grated parmesan cheese
- ½ cup/125 g fresh ricotta cheese
- 1 large egg
- 1½ tablespoons butter
- 1²⁄₃ cups/250 g all-purpose/plain flour
- 2 tablespoons extra-virgin olive oil

Suggested wine: a dry, lightly sparkling red (Lambrusco Salamino di Santa Croce)

Torta di riso con la zucca

Rice and pumpkin pie

Bring the water, milk, and a dash of salt to a boil. Add the rice. Cook for 10 minutes then drain. ▪ Peel the pumpkin. Remove the seeds and grate the raw flesh finely into the center of a clean cloth. Gather up the cloth and twist it round tightly, squeezing some of the moisture out of the pumpkin. ▪ Mix the grated pumpkin with the rice, then add the parmesan, ricotta, egg, butter, salt, and pepper. ▪ Sift the flour into a mound in a mixing bowl and make a well in the center. Pour in the oil and a little water. Gradually mix in the flour, adding water a little at a time, to form an easily worked dough. ▪ Knead the dough until smooth and elastic and then roll out into a thin sheet. ▪ Cut out two disks of pastry, one larger than the other. Use the bigger one to line a 10 in/25 cm diameter pie or cake pan greased with butter and sprinkled with bread crumbs. ▪ Fill with the rice and pumpkin mixture and cover with the other disk of pastry, pinching the edges together to seal. Brush the surface with the oil and prick several times with a fork. ▪ Bake in a preheated oven at 350°F/180°C/gas 4 for about 45 minutes. ▪ Serve hot or at room temperature.

A typical dish from the countryside around Parma.

Piadina: a taste of summer

Simple yet delicious, Romagnol flatbread, known in Italian as *piada* or *piadina*, is made of flour, lard, salt, and water. Its origins go far back into history, probably to Etruscan times (800–300 BC). However, it is also reminiscent of modern peasant breads, such as Turkish *yufta*, Indian *rodha*, Eritrean *burgutta*, and Mexican *tortilla*. In some modern versions baking soda is added with the flour to make the flatbread lighter and easier to digest.

Sometimes olive oil is used instead of lard, and milk or baker's yeast is added, but the essential "ingredient" is the skillful touch of the cook who mixes, kneads, and shapes the piadina. The basic recipe varies according to the city or province: in Rimini thin, light *piada* are preferred; in Ravenna milk, honey, and grated lemon zest are sometimes added; in Cattolica mineral water is used to mix the dough: the list of variations is endless.

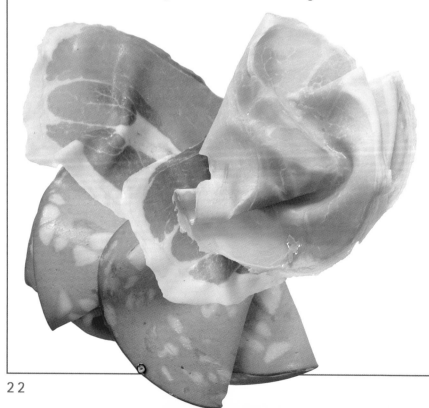

The piadina is one of Italy's answers to fast food. It is eaten hot, with cultivated or wild salad greens (watercress is a favorite) and with fresh, white cow's milk cheeses (such as *squaquarone*, a local specialty) or with goat's or sheep's milk cheese. It is also served with cured meats, such as mortadella, prosciutto, ham, and pork. Flatbread must be eaten as soon as it is cooked: a cold piadina is heavy and hard to digest and loses its appetizing fragrance if reheated. Piadinas are ubiquitous in Romagna, and are served everywhere, from seafront stalls to cafès, to restaurants and roadside eating places.

Italy's famous film director Federico Fellini, born in Rimini, was passionately fond of piadina. To this day, the owners of bars and eating places like to remember how he used to sit down to a hot piadina and a chat with friends.

Most Italians and tourists prefer their piadinas with a ham or cheese filling and accompanied by a glass of full-bodied red Sangiovese wine. The locals, however, who have grown up with piadine, maintain that they should be accompanied by a light white Trebbiano wine.

The Romagnol riviera has something for everyone: many summer vacationers stay in the top class hotels in the area, while backpackers find cheap *pensione* or simply doss down on the warm beaches.

Italians associate flatbread with holidays. The Romagnol riviera (the coast between Cattolica and Ravenna), is one of the most popular summer resort areas in Italy. The people of Romagna are known for their carefree and fun-loving nature, and the piadina is synonymous with late night snacks at food stalls after a walk along the seafront, or after a long night of sampling Romagna's *dolce vita* (such as the all-night discoteques, which are among the most fashionable in Italy).

Erbazzone

Savory pie

Serves: 6
Preparation: 30 minutes
Cooking: 35 minutes
Recipe grading: fairly easy

- 2½ lb/1.2 kg Swiss chard, spinach beet, or spinach leaves
- 5 oz/150 g pancetta
- 2 tablespoons finely chopped parsley
- 1 clove garlic
- 6 scallions/spring onions or shallots
- ¾ cup/90 g freshly grated parmesan cheese
- salt and freshly ground black pepper
- 3⅓ cups/350 g all-purpose/plain flour
- dash of salt
- 4 tablespoons melted lard
- warm water for the dough

Suggested wine: a dry white
(Pomposa Bianco)

Wash the chard or spinach leaves well, but do not dry. Cook with just the water left clinging to the leaves for a few minutes. Squeeze out as much moisture as possible and chop very coarsely. ▪ Chop the pancetta finely with the parsley, garlic, and scallions or shallots. Sauté in a lightly greased skillet (frying pan) until the onion is tender. ▪ Set 1 tablespoon of this mixture aside. Leave the rest in the skillet and add the chopped chard, parmesan, salt, and pepper. Stir well. ▪ Sift the flour and a dash of salt into a mixing bowl. Make a well in the center and pour the melted lard into it. ▪ Gradually stir in the flour, adding a little warm water at intervals, to form an easily worked dough. ▪ Knead the dough until smooth and elastic. ▪ Divide it into two parts, one larger than the other, and roll out into two thin disks. Use the larger one to line a deep, greased 9½ in/24 cm diameter pie pan. It should overlap the edges a little. ▪ Fill with the prepared mixture, then smooth this level. Cover with the other disk, sealing the edges well. ▪ Spread the reserved 1 tablespoon of fried mixture over the surface of the dough. Bake in a preheated oven at 400°F/200°C/gas 6 for 30 minutes. This savory pie is best served warm rather than hot.

Also called scarpazon *or* scarpassa *in Reggio Emilia, its other name* morazzone *comes from the Latin* moretum, *the ancient Romans' very simple, rustic vegetable pie.*

Serves: 4
Preparation: 10 minutes
Recipe grading: easy

- 1 lb/500 g mâche, corn salad, or lamb's lettuce
- 3½ oz/100 g parmesan cheese
- ½ cup/125 ml extra-virgin olive oil
- salt
- 2 tablespoons best quality Modena balsamic vinegar

Insalata all'aceto balsamico

Salad with balsamic vinegar dressing

Wash and dry the mâche, then place it in a salad bowl. ▪ Add the parmesan, in shavings or slivers. ▪ Beat the oil, salt, and balsamic vinegar together in a small, deep bowl until very well blended. ▪ Drizzle over the salad and toss thoroughly. Serve at once.

The salad is really only an excuse for savoring the aroma and flavor of Modena's highly prized balsamic vinegar. You can, of course, vary the amount of oil and of vinegar according to taste.

Gelato di parmigiano

Parmesan cheese ice cream

Mix the cream with the parmesan, salt, and cayenne pepper in the top of a double boiler or in a heatproof bowl. Cook over simmering water until the cheese is completely melted. Remove from the heat and set aside to cool. ▪ Pour through a sieve to strain. ▪ Pour the resulting liquid into an ice cream maker and process as directed. ▪ If you don't have an ice cream maker, pour the liquid into a freezerproof container and freeze, stirring at intervals as the mixture thickens and freezes. ▪ After 3 hours in the freezer, take the mixture out and transfer to a food processor. Blend until smooth, then replace it in the freezer. Repeat this process after another 3 hours' freezing. ▪ Serve with an ice cream scoop or a tablespoon.

Serves: 6
Preparation: about 15 minutes + 6 hours' freezing
Recipe grading: easy

- 2 cups/500 ml light/single cream
- 2¾ cups/350 g freshly grated parmesan cheese
- salt
- dash of cayenne or chile pepper

Suggested wine: a dry or medium, lightly sparkling red (Lambrusco di Sorbara)

This unusual starter used to be served later in the meal, replacing the cheese course. As an appetizer, it goes very well with thin slices of prosciutto (Parma ham).

Torta di patate

Potato pie

Boil the potatoes until tender. Peel them and put through the ricer while still hot. ▪ Chop the onion and pork fat finely. Fry them together in the butter on a low heat in a large, nonstick skillet (frying pan). ▪ Add the roast meat juices or stock and turn off the heat. ▪ Add the potatoes, parmesan, milk, and salt, and stir thoroughly. ▪ Sift the flour with a dash of salt into a mixing bowl. Make a well in the center and add 1 tablespoon of the olive oil and a little warm water. ▪ Gradually mix in the flour, adding water a little at a time, to form an easily worked dough. ▪ Knead the dough until smooth and elastic. ▪ Working with a well-floured rolling pin and pastry board, roll out the dough into a thin sheet. Cut out two disks, one larger than the other. ▪ Use the larger one to line a 9½ in/24 cm diameter deep pie pan or cake pan, greased with butter and sprinkled with fine bread crumbs. ▪ Fill with the potato mixture, then cover with the pastry lid and seal the edges. Brush the surface with the remaining oil and prick several times with a fork. ▪ Bake in a preheated oven at 350°F/180°C/gas 4 for 45 minutes.

Serves: 6–8
Preparation: 45 minutes
Cooking: 45 minutes + 30 minutes for the potatoes
Recipe grading: fairly easy

- 2 lb/1 kg potatoes
- 1 onion
- generous ½ cup/70 g finely chopped fresh pork fat
- 1 tablespoon butter
- 2 tablespoons cooking juices from roast meat or poultry (or stock made with a bouillon cube)
- 1¼ cups/150 g freshly grated parmesan cheese
- 4 tablespoons milk
- salt
- 1⅓ cups/200 g all-purpose/plain flour
- 2 tablespoons extra-virgin olive oil

Suggested wine: a dry, fruity white (Colli Piacentini Sauvignon)

This is one of Piacenza's specialties. For an even tastier version, cook 1 tablespoon of finely chopped fresh rosemary leaves with the onion and pork fat and stir 1 tablespoon of tomato paste into the filling.

Serves: 6
Preparation: 10 minutes
Recipe grading: easy

- 12 slices prosciutto (preferably top-quality Parma ham)
- 1 cantaloupe melon/rock melon and/or 6 fresh, ripe figs

Suggested wine: a dry, lightly sparkling white (Colli Piacentini Pinot Grigio Vivace)

Prosciutto con melone

Prosciutto with melon

Slice the melon lengthwise into 6 wedges and remove the skin, or gently pull open the figs or slice them in half from top to bottom. ▪ Arrange the ham slices in the center of a serving platter. Arrange the melon slices, or figs, around them, or alternate these if using both fruits. Serve.

Parma ham's superb, yet delicate flavor probably makes it the most famous of all Italian cured meats. Served with melon or, on a more rustic note, figs, it is the perfect appetizer for hot summer nights.

Frittatine all'aceto balsamico

Fritters in balsamic vinegar

Sauté the onions in the olive oil until they are light golden brown. ▪ Beat the eggs and a dash of salt together in a bowl. Stir in the parmesan and bread crumbs. ▪ Add the onions and mix well. Set aside for at least 30 minutes. ▪ Drop tablespoonsful of the mixture into plenty of very hot oil and fry until golden brown all over. ▪ Drain the fritters on paper towels. Drizzle with balsamic vinegar to taste and serve very hot.

Serves: 4
Preparation: 15 minutes + at least
    30 minutes' standing
Cooking: 15 minutes
Recipe grading: easy

- ▪ 4 small onions, thinly sliced
- ▪ 4 tablespoons extra-virgin olive oil
- ▪ 4 large eggs
- ▪ dash of salt
- ▪ ½ cup/60 g freshly grated parmesan cheese
- ▪ 4 tablespoons dry bread crumbs
- ▪ oil, for frying
- ▪ balsamic vinegar

Suggested wine: a dry white (Colli Bolognesi
Riesling Italico Asciutto)

*This simple dish exalts the superb flavor of
Modena's wonderful balsamic vinegar.*

Primi piatti

Romagnol stuffed pasta	33
Tortellini in meat stock	35
Stuffed pasta with pumpkin filling	36
Cheese dumpling soup	37
Baked lasagna Bologna-style	38
Pasta and bean soup	43
Pasta with meat sauce and peas	44
Stuffed pasta with cheese filling	48
Rice Piacenza-style	49
Stuffed pasta roll	50
Clam soup	52
Stuffed pasta with spinach and ricotta filling	53
Ribbon noodles with prosciutto	55
Macaroni pie Ferrara-style	56
Eel risotto	58
Risotto with John Dory	59

Emilia is the homeland of fresh, egg-based pasta fatto in casa (homemade). From the same piece of pasta dough, Emilian cooks can turn out a vast array of delicious dishes, including tortellini, lasagne, cappelletti, cappellacci, tagliatelle, maltagliati, and many more. They are often served in tasty boiling stock, but will also appear in a range of meat or vegetable sauces. The stuffed varieties change shape, name, and main filling ingredient according to the town or village where they are made.

Cappelletti di magro romagnoli

Romagnol stuffed pasta

Prepare the pasta dough as explained on page 47. ▪ Shape the dough into a ball and set aside to rest for about 1 hour, wrapped in plastic wrap (cling film). ▪ Mix the cheeses in a bowl with the eggs, nutmeg, and salt. ▪ Roll out the pasta into a thin sheet. Fill and assemble the cappelletti following the instructions for tortellini on page 35. Set aside to rest for about 2 hours. ▪ Add the cappelletti to the boiling stock and simmer for 2–3 minutes. ▪ Serve hot in soup dishes with the stock.

Serves: 4–5
Preparation: 1 hour + 3 hours' total resting for the pasta dough and cappelletti
Cooking: 2–3 minutes
Recipe grading: complicated

- 1 quantity pasta dough (see recipe, page 47)

For the filling:
- ¾ cup/180 g fresh, white soft cheese (stracchino or crescenza)
- ¾ cup/180 g ricotta cheese
- ¾ cup/90 g freshly grated parmesan cheese
- 2 large eggs
- dash of freshly grated nutmeg
- salt
- 1½ quarts/1.5 liters boiling stock (homemade—see recipe, page 77—or bouillon cube)

Suggested wine: a young, dry red (Rubicone Sangiovese)

If you can't get stracchino or crescenza cheese, omit it and double the quantity of ricotta. Cappelletti are traditionally served in boiling stock made from a selection of meat and poultry. Some cooks add half a capon breast, very finely chopped, to this filling.

Tortellini in brodo
Tortellini in meat stock

Prepare the pasta dough as explained on page 47. ▪ Shape the dough into a ball and set aside to rest for about 1 hour, wrapped in plastic wrap (cling film). ▪ Melt the butter in a skillet (frying pan) and gently fry the pork. When cooked, grind it finely with the mortadella and prosciutto. ▪ Transfer the meat mixture to a bowl and mix well with the egg, parmesan, nutmeg, salt, and pepper. (The filling can be prepared a day in advance.) ▪ Roll out the pasta dough on a lightly floured surface to a thickness of ⅛ in/3 mm. Use a plain pastry wheel to cut the pasta sheet into 1¼ in/3 cm squares. ▪ Place a mound of filling (about the size of a marble) in the center of each square. Then bring two opposite corners of the square together to form a triangle, pinching the edges together to seal tightly. Fold the apex of the triangle over slightly and bring the remaining two corners together, bending the tortellino around a finger as if it were a ring. Pinch the two corners tightly to make them hold together, then slide off your finger. As you make the tortellini, spread them out on a clean cloth to dry for about 2 hours. ▪ Add the tortellini to the stock and simmer for 2–3 minutes (if boiled fast, they tend to come apart). ▪ Serve in fairly deep soup dishes, allowing about a tablespoonful of stock for each tortellino.

Serves: 4–5
Preparation: 1 hour + 3 hours' total resting for the pasta dough and tortellini
Cooking: 2 hours
Recipe grading: complicated

- 1 quantity pasta dough (see recipe, page 47)

For the filling:
- 2 tablespoons butter
- 4 oz/125 g lean pork (tenderloin), chopped into small pieces
- 4 oz/125 g mortadella
- 3 oz/90 g prosciutto/Parma ham
- 1 large egg
- 1¾ cups/215 g freshly grated parmesan cheese
- dash of freshly grated nutmeg
- salt and freshly ground black pepper

- 1½ quarts/1.5 liters boiling stock (homemade—see recipe, page 77—or bouillon cube)

Suggested wine: a dry or medium, lightly sparkling red (Lambrusco Grasparossa)

Slightly different versions of these little stuffed pasta packages are known all over Emilia Romagna under various names. Tradition has it that they originated in Bologna. However, despite attempts to end the controversy over the classic recipe by registering the "approved" ingredients with the Bologna Chamber of Commerce, each cook sticks to her own family tradition, leading to an infinite variety of excellent and original fillings. This recipe is most typical of the Bologna area.

Serves: 4–6
Preparation: 1 hour + 3 hours' total resting
  for the pasta dough and cappellacci
Cooking: 30 minutes
Recipe grading: complicated

For the filling:

- 2¾ lb/1.3 kg fresh (or 2 14-oz/
  450-g cans) pumpkin
- 1¾ cups/215 g freshly grated
  parmesan cheese
- 1 large egg
- dash of grated nutmeg
- ½ cup/60 g fine dry bread crumbs
- salt
- 7 tablespoons butter, melted
- 1 quantity pasta dough (see recipe,
  page 47)

Suggested wine: a dry or medium, lightly
sparkling red (Lambrusco di Sorbara)

*The use of pumpkin as a filling originated
at the court of the Dukes of Este in Ferrara,
where its sweet taste was very popular. As
with* tortellini, *many different versions,
with differing names, can be found
throughout most of Emilia Romagna. In
Mantua, to the north in Lombardy, 1 cup/
125 g of finely pounded amaretti cookies
are added to the filling.*

Cappellacci di zucca

Stuffed pasta with pumpkin filling

Without peeling the pumpkin, scrape away the seeds and fibers and cut it into slices 1½ in/4 cm thick. ▪ Bake in a preheated oven at 400°F/200°C/gas 6 until tender. ▪ Remove the flesh from the skin. Sieve the flesh into a mixing bowl while still hot. ▪ Mix well with three-quarters of the parmesan, the egg, nutmeg, bread crumbs, and salt. ▪ Cover the bowl with plastic wrap (cling film) and leave to stand for 2 hours. ▪ Prepare the pasta dough as explained on page 47. ▪ Shape the dough into a ball and set aside to rest for about 1 hour, wrapped in plastic wrap. ▪ Roll out the dough to a thin, almost transparent sheet. Use a fluted pastry wheel to cut into 3 in/7.5 cm squares and place ½ tablespoon of the filling in a mound in the center of each one. Fold and seal the edges by pressing gently with your fingertips. ▪ Simmer in a large pan of boiling water until they bob up to the surface, when they are done. ▪ Serve hot, drizzled with the butter and sprinkled with the remaining parmesan.

Passatelli

Cheese dumpling soup

Mix the parmesan well with the bread crumbs and eggs in a mixing bowl. ▪ Soften the beef marrow by heating it gently in a small saucepan and then combine with the bread crumbs. ▪ Add the nutmeg, lemon zest, and salt and set aside for 30 minutes. ▪ Press the mixture through a food mill, fitted with the disk with the largest holes, to produce short, cylindrical dumplings, about 1½ in/4 cm long. Cut them off with the tip of a sharp knife as they are squeezed out of the mill. If the mixture is too stiff, add a little broth; if too soft, add some more bread crumbs. ▪ Let the little worm-shaped dumplings fall directly into a saucepan of boiling stock and simmer until they bob up to the surface. ▪ Turn off the heat. Leave to stand for a few minutes and then serve. Traditionally, extra grated parmesan cheese is not served with the dumplings.

Serves: 4–6
Preparation: 25 minutes + 30 minutes' resting for the dumpling mixture
Cooking: 4–5 minutes
Recipe grading: easy

- 1 cup/125 g freshly grated parmesan cheese
- 1¼ cups/150 g very fine dry bread crumbs (not toasted)
- 3 large eggs
- 1 oz/30 g beef marrow or, if preferred, butter
- dash of freshly grated nutmeg
- finely grated zest of 1 lemon
- salt
- 1½ quarts/1.5 liters beef stock (homemade or bouillon cube)

Suggested wine: a dry, fruity white (Colli Piacentini Chardonnay)

Although a Romagnol specialty, this soup is served throughout Emilia Romagna.

Serves: 4–6
Preparation: 30 minutes + 1 hour's resting
   for the pasta
Cooking: 1½ hours
Recipe grading: fairly easy

- generous 1 cup/250 g cooked, drained spinach
- 1 quantity pasta dough (see recipe, page 47)
- 1 quantity meat sauce (see recipe, page 40)

For the Béchamel sauce:
- 4 tablespoons butter
- 4 tablespoons all-purpose/plain flour
- 2 cups/500 ml hot milk

- salt
- 1 tablespoon extra-virgin olive oil
- dash of freshly grated nutmeg
- 2½ cups/300 g freshly grated parmesan cheese
- 1½ tablespoons butter

Suggested wine: a young full-bodied red
(Sangiovese di Romagna)

Lasagne alla bolognese

Baked lasagna Bologna-style

Squeeze as much moisture out of the cooked spinach as possible and chop very finely.
■ Prepare the pasta dough as explained on page 47, incorporating the very finely chopped spinach into the dough with the eggs. ■ Shape the dough into a ball and set aside to rest for about 1 hour, wrapped in plastic wrap (cling film). ■ Prepare the meat sauce. ■ Roll the pasta dough out and cut into rectangles measuring 6 in/15 cm by 4 in/10 cm. ■ To prepare the Béchamel sauce: melt the butter and stir in the flour. ■ Remove from the heat and gradually add the hot milk while stirring continuously. Return to a very low heat and continue stirring with a wooden spoon as the sauce cooks for about 5 minutes. ■ Bring a very large saucepan of water to a boil, then add the salt and the tablespoon of oil (to prevent the sheets of lasagna from sticking to one another). Add the lasagna and cook for 2–3 minutes. ■ Drain the lasagna and spread them out on clean, dry cloths to dry off for a few minutes. ■ Spoon a thin layer of the meat sauce over the bottom of a fairly deep, rectangular ovenproof dish and cover with a layer of lasagna. Spread with a layer of Béchamel and sprinkle with parmesan. Repeat this process until all the ingredients are used up. The top layer should be lasagna, covered with Béchamel sauce and sprinkled with the remaining parmesan. ■ Dot with the last measure of butter and bake in a preheated oven at 375°F/190°C/gas 5 for 30 minutes. ■ Leave to stand for 5 minutes before serving.

This type of pasta, the oldest after gnocchi, is made in many regions of Italy, where it is known variously as lagane, vincigrassi, *and* sagne. *There are two types of lasagna: the long, ribbon type, called* pappardelle, *and the thicker, rectangular ones, 4–6 in/10–15 cm long and at least 2½ in/6–7 cm wide, which are usually baked in the oven with various fillings and sauces. This classic recipe, made with spinach, is a traditional Bolognese dish.*

Parmesan cheese

Widely known as the "champagne" of cheeses, parmesan is historically so rooted in the Italian way of life as to merit a place in Boccaccio's *Decameron*. The origins of this cheese are lost in the mists of time, but it is fairly safe to say that parmesan was first made in medieval monasteries. Parts of the granaries and cowsheds were set aside for milk processing and subsequently evolved into cheese dairies. In what was known as the milk room, the monks probably experimented with making the forerunners of parmesan. They discovered that by double "cooking" the milk, that is heating it twice and controlling the temperature, an even greater concentration of the protein content could be obtained, resulting in a firm textured cheese with very little watery residue.

Parmesan is produced in the provinces of Parma, Reggio Emilia, Modena, and Bologna (and also in Mantua, which is part of Lombardy). However, according to Italian law, only the manufacturers located in the provinces of Parma, Modena, and Reggio Emilia may adopt the denomination of "*parmigiano reggiano*," which is the best parmesan. Producers outside this zone must label their cheese as "grana."

Meat Sauce
For six, to serve with pasta

1 onion, finely chopped
1 carrot, finely chopped
1 stalk celery, finely chopped
2 tablespoons butter
1 cup/250 g finely ground lean pork
1 cup/250 g finely ground lean beef
½ cup/150 g trimmed chicken livers, ground
1 cup/250 ml dry red wine
1¼ cups/310 g peeled and chopped fresh or
    canned tomatoes
salt and freshly ground pepper to taste

Sauté the onion, carrot, and celery in the butter in a large heavy-bottomed saucepan. Add the pork, beef, and chicken livers, moisten with the wine and cook until it has evaporated. Stir in the tomatoes and salt and pepper to taste. Cover and leave to simmer gently for at least 50 minutes.

Authentic parmesan is made only from the milk of cows who have foraged outdoors, so that it is completely free of additives. It is made during the summer months, from May to October. After being salted, a process that takes about 30 days, it is matured in large cylindrical forms for at least a year, until the end of the summer after it was made. Some very special types are matured for several years and are known as *stravecchi* (extremely old). Over 1000 pounds (500 kg) of cow's milk are needed to make just one form of cheese.

Parmesan makes an excellent companion to *spumante* (sparkling wine) or *vino frizzante* (semi-sparkling wine), such as Lambrusco. It makes a delicious appetizer and also goes well with any number of first courses. Before the tomato was introduced into Europe, parmesan was the preferred compliment to pasta throughout Italy. Parmesan should be kept in the refrigerator wrapped in a linen or cotton cloth to preserve the aroma and taste while preventing the development of undesirable mold.

There are many historical references to parmesan. Records from Renaissance times show that it was exported to Constantinople, Paris, Vienna, and London. Even earlier, in Giovanni Boccaccio's Decameron, one of the tales describes a mountain of parmesan in the land of Bengodi (a metaphor for "land of pleasures") on the top of which industrious people are busy creating ravioli and tortelli.

Parmesan is a hard cheese with a slow maturation process. It is made by curdling milk which is partially skimmed halfway through the coagulating process; a certain quantity of whey left over from the preceding batch is then added to these curds. The same production methods have been used for over 700 years.

Malmaritati

Pasta and bean soup

Prepare the pasta dough as explained on page 47. ▪ Shape the dough into a ball and set aside to rest for about 1 hour, wrapped in plastic wrap (cling film). ▪ Roll out the dough into a thin sheet. Cut into uneven diamond shapes by first cutting it diagonally into strips, then cutting in the opposite direction. (In the past, when fresh pasta was made every day, leftover pieces and offcuts of pasta were used for maltagliati). ▪ Place the beans in a deep saucepan with enough cold water to cover. Then add the onion, carrot, celery, but no salt at this stage. Bring to a boil and simmer gently for about 2 hours. ▪ When the beans are very tender, press half of them through a sieve and add salt to taste. Reserve the remaining beans and the cooking liquid. ▪ Sauté the garlic in the oil in a large, heavy-bottomed pan until it starts to color, then discard it. ▪ Add the parsley and tomatoes to the flavored oil. Cook, uncovered, to reduce and thicken. Then add the bean purée, the whole beans, and the cooking liquid. ▪ Bring this thick soup to a boil, then add the maltagliati. They will take 3–4 minutes to cook. ▪ Serve hot, adding a trickle of extra-virgin olive oil and a sprinkling of parmesan to each serving.

Serves: 4–6
Preparation: 30 minutes + 1 hour's resting for the pasta
Cooking: 2½ hours
Recipe grading: fairly easy

For the maltagliati pasta:
- ¾ quantity pasta dough (see recipe, page 47)

For the soup:
- 1½ cups/300 g dried and soaked, (or 2 lb/1 kg fresh) borlotti or red kidney beans
- 1 small onion, peeled
- 1 carrot, trimmed and peeled
- 1 stalk celery, trimmed and washed
- salt
- 1 clove garlic, peeled and lightly crushed
- ½ cup/125 ml extra-virgin olive oil + extra to serve
- 1 tablespoon finely chopped parsley
- scant 1 cup/200 g fresh or canned Italian tomatoes, sieved
- 2 tablespoons freshly grated parmesan cheese

Suggested wine: a young dry red (Rubicone Sangiovese)

Maltagliati (literally "badly cut" pasta) are the main ingredient of this recipe. They are popular throughout Emilia Romagna and are also used in minestrone. Served hot, this bean soup makes a hearty first course for cold winter nights. It is also very good in summertime, served cold. If you don't have time to make fresh pasta, use dried ditalini *pasta instead. The* ditalini *should be cooked in boiling, salted water until just tender and then added to the bean soup. For extra taste, add 1 tablespoon of finely chopped fresh, young rosemary leaves at the same time as the parsley and tomatoes.*

Serves: 4–6
Preparation: 45 minutes + 1 hour's resting
  for the pasta
Cooking: about 1 hour
Recipe grading: fairly easy

- 1 quantity pasta dough
  (see recipe, page 47)
- 2 tablespoons freshly grated
  parmesan cheese
- dash of freshly grated nutmeg
- dash of salt

- 1 quantity meat sauce
  (see recipe, page 40)
- ¾ cup/100 g fresh or frozen peas

Suggested wine: a young, dry red
(Rubicone Sangiovese)

Garganelli con ragù e pisellini

Pasta with meat sauce and peas

Prepare the pasta dough as explained on page 47, incorporating the parmesan, nutmeg, and salt with the eggs. ▪ Shape the dough into a ball and set aside to rest for about 1 hour, wrapped in plastic wrap (cling film). ▪ Prepare the meat sauce, adding the peas 10 minutes before the sauce is done. ▪ Roll out the dough until very thin. Use a smooth-edged pastry wheel or a knife to cut the pasta sheet into 2½ in/6–7 cm squares. ▪ To shape the garganelli, place a large comb flat on the work surface, teeth facing away from you. Place a pasta square diagonally on the largest teeth with a corner pointing toward you; put the pencil across this corner, parallel with the comb, and roll up the square onto it, pushing down on the comb's teeth as you roll it away from you. Slide the garganello off the pencil. ▪ Add the garganelli to a large saucepan of boiling salted water and cook gently for 5 minutes or less. ▪ Drain well, then toss carefully with the meat sauce and serve. ▪ Garganelli are also very good when served in boiling homemade meat or vegetable stock.

Garganelli are a specialty of Lugo di Romagna. Their name is derived from the Romagnol dialect word for a chicken gizzard, which is suggested by the distinctive pattern of horizontal grooves made by pressing them against the teeth of a wool weaver's comb. Italian cooks use a special utensil, a 4 x 10 in/ 10 x 25 cm wooden frame with thin wires running across it, and a smooth, pencil-size wooden dowel around which the pasta squares are wrapped. A very clean, large-toothed comb and a pencil can be used instead.

Fresh Pasta

Eating lies at the very heart of life in Emilia Romagna and, predictably, the region's cooking is full of hearty and distinctive flavors and aromas which come together to make dishes that are nothing less than works of art. The alluring smoothness and taste of freshly made pasta, plain or stuffed, served in simple butter and herb or meat sauces, or broth, are surely among the most remarkable of the region's offerings. Fresh pasta, or *pasta fatta in casa* (homemade), owes its fame to the dough, a simple mixture of eggs, flour, salt, and water to which the typical Emilian woman (this is traditionally a female art) then applies her rolling pin with passion and precision, until it is transformed into a very thin sheet of pasta.

Tagliatelle

Tagliatelle are the simplest type of fresh pasta. They made their first documented appearance in an account of the marriage banquet of Lucrezia Borgia and the Duke of Ferrara in the second half of the sixteenth century. Lucrezia's long, blond tresses are said to have provided the inspiration for the cook who created them, a certain Master Zafirano. *Tagliatelle* are a Bolognese specialty, and are traditionally served with ragù, the rich meat sauce which also traces its origins to the city. Legend has it that *tortellini* were invented by an innkeeper who, in a frenzy of passion after spying through the keyhole on a beautiful lady undressing (perhaps Venus herself!), was inspired to copy the shape of her navel using pasta dough. Small *tortellini*, filled with meat (pork, chicken, and prosciutto) are typical of Bologna, but many other towns in Emilia have their own versions. In Piacenza and Parma they are called anolini and the main ingredient of the filling is braised beef; in Reggio Emilia they are called *cappelletti* and are stuffed with veal, beef, pork, or prosciutto, while in Ferrara they are slightly larger and called *cappellacci*. They are traditionally served in broth or with ragù.

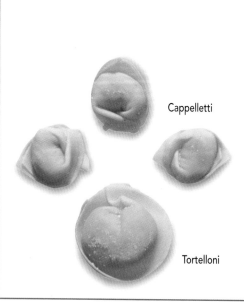

Cappelletti

Tortelloni

Tortellini

Making your own pasta at home can be fun and gratifying. To get started, make sure you have a long, thin rolling pin, made of hardwood. In Emilia these measure up to 58 in (1½ meters) in length and have a maximum diameter of 2 in (5 cm). You will also need a pastry board, preferably absolutely level and made of softwood. A pastry wheel and a sharp knife with a long, straight blade will also prove helpful.

Mixing plain pasta dough
For 4 generous servings you will need 2⅔ cups/400 g of all-purpose/plain flour and 4 medium eggs. Place the flour in a mound on a flat work surface and hollow out a well in the center. Break the eggs into the well one by one. Stir gently with a fork, gradually incorporating the flour. When the mixture is no longer runny, use your hands to finish combining the flour with the eggs. Work the mixture with your hands until it is smooth and moist, but quite firm.

To test the mixture for the correct consistency, press a clean finger into the dough. If it comes out without any dough sticking to it, it is ready for kneading. If it is too moist, add more flour. If it is too dry, incorporate a little milk. Roll the mixture into a ball shape.

Kneading the dough
Clean the work surface of any excess dough and lightly sprinkle with flour. Push down and forwards on the ball of pasta dough with the heel of your palm. Fold the slightly extended piece of dough in half, give it a quarter-turn, and repeat.

Continue for about 10 minutes or until the dough is very smooth. Place the ball of pasta dough on a plate and cover with an upturned bowl. Leave to rest for at least 15–20 minutes.

Rolling the dough out by hand
Place the ball of dough on a flat, clean work surface and flatten it a little with your hand. Place the rolling pin on the center of the flattened ball and, applying light but firm pressure, roll the dough away from you. Give the ball a quarter-turn and repeat. When the dough has become a large round about ¼ in/5 mm thick, curl the far edge over the pin while holding the edge closest to you with your hand. Gently stretch the pasta as you roll it all onto the pin. Unroll, give the dough a quarter-turn, and repeat. Continue rolling and stretching the dough until it is transparent.

Rolling the dough out using the pasta machine
Divide the dough in to several pieces and flatten them slightly with your hand. Set the machine with its rollers at their widest, and run each piece through the machine. Reduce the rollers' width by one notch and repeat, reducing the rollers' width by one notch each time. Continue until all the pieces have gone through the machine at the thinnest roller setting.

Serves: 4–6
Preparation: 45 minutes + 1 hour's resting for the pasta
Cooking: 10 minutes
Recipe grading: fairly easy

- ½ quantity pasta dough (see recipe, page 47)

For the filling:

- scant ⅔ cup/150 g mild, soft white cheese (squaquarone, crescenza, robiola, or ricotta)
- ¾ cup/90 g freshly grated parmesan cheese
- 2 large eggs
- salt
- 1½ quarts/1.5 liters beef stock (homemade or bouillon cube)

Suggested wine: a young, dry red (Rubicone Sangiovese)

Pasta ripiena alla brisighellese

Stuffed pasta with cheese filling

Prepare the pasta dough as explained on page 47. ▪ Shape the dough into a ball and set aside to rest for about 1 hour, wrapped in plastic wrap (cling film). ▪ Mix the fresh white cheese in a bowl with the parmesan, eggs, and a dash of salt. ▪ Roll out the pasta dough into a very thin sheet. Cover half its surface with the cheese mixture, spreading it out evenly. ▪ Fold the other half of the dough over the top and roll lightly with a rolling pin to ensure that the layers stick firmly together. ▪ Use a fluted pastry wheel to cut into ¾ in/2 cm squares. ▪ Add the pasta to the boiling stock and simmer for 10 minutes. ▪ Serve very hot.

Bomba di riso alla piacentina

Rice Piacenza-style

Wash the squab inside and out and pat dry with paper towels. Cut into 5 or 6 pieces. ▪ Sauté the onion in half the butter in a heavy-bottomed pan for a few minutes. ▪ Add the sage leaves and squab, then brown the meat well all over. ▪ Pour in the wine and cook, uncovered, until the wine has reduced. Season with salt and pepper. ▪ Stir in the tomato paste and water. Cover and simmer over a low heat for about 20 minutes, stirring now and then. ▪ Cook the rice for 8 minutes in a large pan of boiling, salted water until tender. ▪ Drain and transfer to a large bowl. Stir in the juices from the squab, the eggs, parmesan, and half the remaining butter. ▪ Grease the inside of a bombe mold or large ovenproof bowl with the rest of the butter. Sprinkle with the bread crumbs, tipping out any excess. ▪ Use two-thirds of the rice mixture to line the mold, pressing firmly to make sure it stays in place. Arrange the pieces of squab in the middle of the mold. Cover with the remaining rice and sprinkle with the remaining bread crumbs. ▪ Bake in a preheated oven at 350°F/180°C/gas 4 for 40 minutes. ▪ Remove from the oven and leave to stand for 10 minutes. Turn out carefully onto a heated plate and serve.

Serves: 4–6
Preparation: 40 minutes
Cooking: about 1 hour
Recipe grading: fairly easy

- a cleaned, oven-ready plump young squab/Cornish hen/pigeon
- 1 onion, very thinly sliced
- 7 tablespoons butter
- 2 leaves fresh sage
- ½ cup/125 ml dry white wine
- salt and freshly ground black pepper
- 1 teaspoon tomato paste dissolved in ½ cup/125 ml cold water
- 2½ cups/500 g Italian risotto rice (Arborio)
- 2 large eggs
- ½ cup/60 g freshly grated parmesan cheese
- ½ cup/60 g fine bread crumbs

Suggested wine: a dry, lightly sparkling red (Lambrusco Reggiano)

In Piacenza this dish is traditionally served on August 15 to celebrate the Feast of the Assumption of the Virgin Mary

Serves: 4–6
Preparation: 1 hour + 1 hour's resting
    for the pasta
Cooking: about 1½ hours
Recipe grading: complicated

- 1 quantity pasta dough (see recipe, page 47)

For the filling:
- 2 lb/1 kg spinach leaves
- generous ¾ cup/180 g butter
- scant 1 cup/100 g freshly grated parmesan cheese
- 7 oz/200 g fresh mushrooms, thinly sliced, or ⅔ cup/45 g dried Italian porcini mushrooms, soaked in warm water and drained
- 1⅓ cups/200 g trimmed chicken livers
- scant ½ cup/100 g fresh Italian sausage meat
- 1¾ cups/200 g finely ground lean veal
- salt

Suggested wine: a dry red (Sangiovese)

Rotolo ripieno
Stuffed pasta roll

Prepare the pasta dough as explained on page 47. ▪ Shape the dough into a ball and set aside to rest for 1 hour, wrapped in plastic wrap (cling film). ▪ Roll out the dough to a thin, rectangular sheet measuring 12 x 16 in/30 cm x 40 cm and cover with a clean cloth or plastic wrap to prevent it drying out. ▪ Wash the spinach leaves thoroughly. Place in a saucepan and cook until tender with just the water left clinging to the leaves. ▪ Squeeze out as much liquid as possible, then chop coarsely. ▪ Sauté the spinach in 2 tablespoons of the butter and stir in 1 tablespoon of the parmesan. ▪ Sauté the mushrooms in 2 tablespoons of the butter for 4–5 minutes. ▪ Poach the chicken livers in a little water. Drain and chop finely. ▪ Melt 4 tablespoons of the remaining butter in a saucepan. Fry the sausage meat over a low heat with the chicken livers and veal. Season with salt and cook for 10 minutes, moistening with a little water if necessary. ▪ Spread this mixture over the sheet of pasta dough, stopping about ¾ in/2 cm short of the edges. Cover with an even layer of spinach, followed by a layer of mushrooms. ▪ Fold over the edge of one of the longer sides and roll up, forming a long sausage. ▪ Wrap tightly in a large piece of cheesecloth. Tie the gathered ends of the cloth with string. ▪ Place the roll in boiling water in an oval casserole (a rectangular fish kettle is ideal). Simmer gently for 50 minutes. ▪ Remove from the water carefully and set aside to cool a little. Then untie and remove the cloth. ▪ Cut into ½ in/1 cm thick slices (like a jelly/swiss roll) and place in a heated ovenproof dish. Melt the remaining butter and pour over the slices, then sprinkle with the parmesan. ▪ Bake in a preheated oven at 475°F/240°C/gas 9 for 5 minutes to brown if wished.

This recipe recurs throughout the region, but the filling varies. This is the most traditional version and comes from Romagna. For an alternative filling, replace the veal, sausage meat, and chicken liver mixture with 2 cups/ 500 g ricotta cheese. Combine this with the spinach, parmesan, and seasoning.

Serves: 4–6
Preparation: 30 minutes + 1–2 hours'
    soaking for the clams
Cooking: 25 minutes
Recipe grading: easy

- 2¾ lb/1.3 kg small clams in their shells
- 3 cloves garlic, peeled and crushed
- ½ cup/125 ml extra-virgin olive oil
- scant 1¼ cups/300 g peeled and coarsely chopped fresh or canned tomatoes
- salt and freshly ground black pepper
- ½ cup/125 ml dry white wine
- 5 thick slices coarse white bread, toasted
- 3 tablespoons finely chopped parsley

Suggested wine: a dry white
(Albana di Romagna)

Zuppa di poveracce

Clam soup

Soak the clams in cold water for 1–2 hours so that any sand they contain will drain away. ▪ Rinse the clams in plenty of cold water, discarding any that remain open. ▪ Sauté the garlic in the oil in a large heavy-bottomed saucepan for 1–2 minutes. Add the tomatoes, then season with salt and pepper. Simmer for 10 minutes. ▪ Add the clams, then cover and cook for a few minutes, until they have all opened (discard any which do not open at this stage). ▪ Pour in the wine and simmer for 10 minutes more. ▪ Arrange the toasted bread in individual soup bowls and ladle the clam soup over the top. Sprinkle with the parsley and serve immediately.

Poveracce are very small, tasty clams which are found all the year round in the Adriatic Sea.

Tortelli alle erbette

Stuffed pasta with spinach and ricotta filling

Prepare the pasta dough as explained on page 47. ▪ Shape the dough into a ball and set aside to rest for about 1 hour, wrapped in plastic wrap (cling film). ▪ Cook the spinach in a little salted water until tender. Drain well, squeeze out the excess moisture, and chop finely. ▪ Combine the spinach, ricotta, egg, half the parmesan, salt, and nutmeg together in a bowl. ▪ Roll out the pasta dough into a very thin sheet. Cut into strips about 6 in/15 cm wide. ▪ Use a teaspoon to place blobs of filling at 2 in/ 5–6 cm intervals along one half of each strip. Fold the half of the strip without filling over the top, then seal along the edges with your fingertips. ▪ Use a pastry wheel to cut between each little package and seal down the edges using a fork. ▪ Cook in a large pan of salted, boiling water with a little olive oil in it to stop the tortelli from sticking together, for about 4–5 minutes. ▪ Drain carefully and serve hot, drizzled with the butter and sprinkled with the remaining parmesan.

Serves: 4–6
Preparation: 30 minutes + 1 hour's resting
  for the pasta
Cooking: 25 minutes
Recipe grading: fairly easy

▪ 1 quantity pasta dough (see recipe, page 47)

For the filling:

▪ 14 oz/400 g fresh spinach leaves
▪ 1¼ cups/310 g ricotta cheese
▪ 1 large egg
▪ 1¾ cups/215 g freshly grated parmesan cheese
▪ salt
▪ dash of freshly ground nutmeg
▪ 7 tablespoons butter, melted

Suggested wine: a dry, fruity white (Pinot Bianco Colli Piacentini)

Tagliatelle al prosciutto
Ribbon noodles with prosciutto

Prepare the pasta dough as explained on page 47. ▪ Shape the dough into a ball and set aside to rest for about 1 hour, wrapped in plastic wrap (cling film). ▪ Roll out the dough to a very thin sheet. Roll the sheet of pasta up loosely, like a thin, rather flattened jelly (swiss) roll 3 in/6–7 cm in diameter. Cut the roll into ¼ in/5 mm thick slices. Unravel the long strips of pasta and spread them out to dry a little (they should not harden). ▪ You will use both the fat and lean of the prosciutto, but cut the fat away from the lean meat and chop both, separately, into tiny dice. ▪ Melt the butter in a large heavy-bottomed saucepan. Sauté the diced fat over a low heat for about 15 minutes before adding the diced lean meat. Cook for 5 minutes more, then season with salt and pepper. Remove from the heat. ▪ Bring a large pan of salted water to a boil (allow 4½ cups/1 liter for every 3–4 oz/100 g of fresh pasta, plus an extra 4½ cups/1 liter). Cook the tagliatelle for 4–5 minutes. ▪ Drain well, but reserve 1 cup/250 ml of the cooking water separately. ▪ Add the tagliatelle to the saucepan with the prosciutto. Return to a fairly high heat and cook for 1–2 minutes, adding a little of the reserved water to moisten, if necessary. ▪ Sprinkle with parmesan and serve at once.

Serves: 4–6
Preparation: 40 minutes + 1 hour's resting for the pasta
Cooking: 30 minutes
Recipe grading: fairly easy

▪ 1 quantity pasta dough (see recipe, page 47)

For the sauce:
▪ 7 oz/200 g thickly sliced prosciutto/ Parma ham
▪ 6 tablespoons butter
▪ salt and freshly ground black pepper
▪ ½ cup/60 g freshly grated parmesan cheese

Suggested wine: a dry red (Sangiovese)

Of all the forms of fresh pasta, tagliatelle or ribbon noodles are the easiest to make and the most versatile to serve. Their name comes from the verb tagliare, "to cut," as the sheet of pasta is cut into long strips. Classic tagliatelle should be ¼ in/5 mm wide and as thin as practicable. Tagliatelle are also delicious served with meat sauce (see recipe, page 40) or with a simple tomato sauce made by simmering 1½ cups/ 400 ml of sieved tomatoes (passata) with 6 tablespoons butter, ¾ cup/125 g diced prosciutto, and salt and pepper for 20 minutes.

Serves: 4–6
Preparation: 1 hour + 30 minutes' chilling
Cooking: about 1 hour
Recipe grading: complicated

For the pastry:
- 2 cups/300 g all-purpose/plain flour
- salt
- ¼ cup/50 g superfine/caster sugar
- ⅔ cup/150 g butter, chopped
- 3 large egg yolks

For the meat sauce:
- 4 tablespoons butter
- ½ cup/60 g finely chopped pancetta
- 1¾ cups/200 g finely diced veal
- 1 cup/150 g diced chicken livers
- ½ cup/125 ml dry red wine
- 1¼ cups/310 ml sieved tomatoes/passata
- dash of ground cinnamon
- dash of grated nutmeg
- salt and freshly ground pepper to taste

- 1 quantity Béchamel sauce (see recipe, page 38)

- 1 tablespoon butter
- ½ cup/60 g fine dry bread crumbs
- 14 oz/400 g macaroni
- scant 1 cup/100 g freshly grated parmesan cheese

Suggested wine: a dry red (Sangiovese)

Pasticcio alla ferrarese
Macaroni pie Ferrara-style

Sift the flour into a large mixing bowl and stir in a dash of salt and the sugar. Rub the butter into the flour, work quickly using the tips of your fingers. The mixture will look like very fine bread crumbs. ▪ Mix the egg yolks in with a fork, then work briefly by hand, just enough to amalgamate the mixture. ▪ Shape the dough into a ball. Wrap in plastic wrap (cling film). Place in the refrigerator for 30 minutes. ▪ To prepare the meat sauce; melt the butter in a heavy-bottomed pan. Sauté the pancetta for 3–5 minutes. Add the veal and chicken livers, then brown, stirring all the time. ▪ Pour in the wine and cook until it has evaporated. ▪ Add the sieved tomatoes and season with the cinnamon, nutmeg, salt and pepper. ▪ Simmer for 40 minutes over a low heat. ▪ Prepare the Béchamel sauce, following the method on page 38. ▪ Grease a 9½ in/ 24 cm diameter springform pan with the remaining butter and sprinkle with the bread crumbs. ▪ Roll out two-thirds of the pastry dough into a round large enough to line the bottom and sides of the springform pan then line the pan with it. ▪ Cook the macaroni in a large pot of boiling, salted water until they are only just tender and still firm to the bite. ▪ Drain and mix with half the meat sauce. ▪ Spoon a layer of macaroni over the pastry. Cover with a layer of the remaining meat sauce, followed by a layer of béchamel sauce. Sprinkle with a little parmesan. ▪ Repeat the process until you have used up all the ingredients. ▪ Roll out the remaining pastry into a disk to form a lid for the pie. Pinch the edges to seal tightly, enclosing the contents. ▪ Bake in a preheated oven at 350°F/180°C/gas 4 for 35 minutes. ▪ Remove from the oven and leave to stand for 10 minutes before serving.

Dating from Renaissance times, this elaborate dish is still served on special occasions. The combination of slightly sweet pastry and savory filling is typical of Renaissance cuisine.

Serves: 4–6
Preparation: 45 minutes
Cooking: 1 hour
Recipe grading: fairly easy

- 1 eel, weighing about 1¾ lb/800 g
- 1 carrot, peeled and cut into large pieces
- 1 onion, peeled
- 1 stalk celery, trimmed, washed, and cut into pieces
- ¾ cup/45 g finely chopped parsley
- 1 clove garlic, finely chopped
- 3 tablespoons butter
- 2 tablespoons extra-virgin olive oil
- 2 cups/400 g Italian risotto rice
- 4 tablespoons sieved tomatoes/passata
- salt

Suggested wine: a young dry red
(Rubicone Sangiovese)

Risotto all'anguilla
Eel risotto

Have the eel prepared (skinned and trimmed, with head removed) by your fishmonger. Cook the eel with the carrot, onion, and celery according to the method for John Dory given on page 59. ▪ Remove the cooked eel flesh from the bone and chop coarsely. Save all the cooking liquid. ▪ Sauté the parsley and garlic in half the butter and half the oil. Add the rice and cook for a few minutes, stirring continuously. ▪ Pour in about 2 cups/500 ml of the cooking liquid from the eel. Add the rice and cook, stirring frequently, for about 20 minutes or until tender, adding more broth if needed. Season with salt. ▪ While the rice is cooking, drain the onion used to flavor the broth and cut into thin slices. Heat the remaining butter and oil in a saucepan and fry the onion until tender. ▪ Add the chopped eel flesh. Cook briefly before adding the sieved tomatoes and 1 cup/250 ml of the eel liquid. Simmer for 10 minutes. ▪ Stir the eel into the rice and serve immediately with parmesan or another mature grating cheese, passed round separately. ▪ If liked, a little finely grated lemon peel can be stirred into the risotto just before serving.

This risotto is typical of the Comacchio area, where eels are farmed on a large scale in lagoons. Traditionally, it was cooked in seagull's breast stock when the occasional bird was shot during the fall months. A light meat stock can be used instead of the eel stock, but it will not have the same distinctive flavor as the original (which, admittedly, is a somewhat acquired taste).

Risotto col pesce San Pietro

Risotto with John Dory

Clean and trim the fish, reserving the liver if it is still in place. Place the fish in a fish kettle or large saucepan with the carrot, celery, and onion. Add sufficient cold water to completely cover it. Heat the water slowly to a very gentle simmer and poach the fish for 30 minutes. ▪ Sauté the parsley and garlic for a few minutes in half the butter and half the olive oil over a low heat in a wide, heavy bottomed saucepan. ▪ Add the rice and cook for a few minutes, stirring continuously. ▪ Pour in 2 cups/500 ml of strained hot cooking liquid from the fish and cook, stirring at frequent intervals; add a little more of the hot, strained fish broth if needed. The rice should be tender after 20 minutes. ▪ Take the onion used to flavor the fish and chop it finely. Sauté the onion gently in the remaining butter and oil. ▪ Add the finely chopped fish liver, if available, and cook briefly. ▪ Add the sieved tomatoes and ¾ cup/180 ml of the fish broth. Simmer, uncovered, over a low heat for 10 minutes. ▪ Sprinkle the risotto with the fish and tomato sauce, and serve. The skinned and filleted fish can be served with the risotto as a meal in itself, or reserved and served as the main course.

Serves: 4–6
Preparation: 1 hour
Cooking: 1 hour
Recipe grading: fairly easy

- a large John Dory fish, weighing about 2 lb/1 kg
- 1 carrot, peeled and cut into large pieces
- 1 stalk celery, trimmed, washed and cut into pieces
- 1 onion, peeled
- 1 cup/60 g finely chopped parsley
- 1 clove garlic, finely chopped
- 6 tablespoons butter
- scant ½ cup/100 ml extra-virgin olive oil
- 2 cups/400 g Italian risotto rice
- 4 tablespoons sieved tomatoes/passata
- salt

Suggested wine: a light, dry white
(Trebbiano di Romagna)

Fish risottos are very popular in the coastal area of Romagna. Any non-oily fish without many small bones is suitable for this dish, provided it has the flavor to make a good broth.

Secondi piatti

Bolognese cutlets	61
Adriatic seafood soup	62
Roast pork Reggio-style	64
Veal cutlets Parma-style	65
Veal rolls	67
Hunter's chicken	70
Calf's liver with balsamic vinegar	71
Roast stuffed capon	73
Chilled veal and ham mold	74
Stuffed pig's trotter with lentils	79
Fried eggy bread with cheese and prosciutto	81
Cotechino sausage with beef and vegetables	82
Stewed eel Comacchio-style	83
Stuffed broiled shrimp	86
Braised red mullet	87

The people of Emilia Romagna have a reputation as lovers of fine dining. A study in the early 1970s discovered that the people of the town of Brisighella were consuming a daily average of 5,500 calories each. This is about twice the daily requirement! While some changes have been made in the meantime, they continue to eat traditional fare, including a wide range of rich meat and fish dishes. This chapter presents a selection of some of the most typical dishes, from both the inland plains and the Adriatic coast.

Cotolette alla bolognese

Bolognese cutlets

Beat the egg lightly in a shallow dish with a dash of salt. ▪ Dip the slices of veal into the egg and then coat all over with the bread crumbs, pressing them so that they adhere well. ▪ Fry the coated veal in hot butter until the slices are golden brown on both sides. ▪ Arrange the veal in a single layer in a very wide skillet (frying pan) or flameproof casserole. Place a slice of prosciutto on each and cover with the parmesan shavings. ▪ Mix the sieved tomatoes with the meat stock and pour into the dish or pan. Cover and simmer for about 15 minutes, until the cheese has completely melted. ▪ Serve immediately.

Serves: 4–6
Preparation: 20 minutes
Cooking: 25 minutes
Recipe grading: easy

- 1 large egg
- dash of salt
- 6 thin slices of veal, taken from a boned leg (escalopes)
- 1 cup/125 g fine dry bread crumbs
- ½ cup/125 g butter
- 6 thin slices of prosciutto/Parma ham
- scant 1 cup/100 g small shavings of parmesan cheese
- scant 1 cup/200 ml sieved tomatoes/passata
- ½ cup/125 ml meat stock (homemade or bouillon cube)

Suggested wine: a dry red
(Colli Bolognesi Cabernet Sauvignon)

This dish is made with two ingredients which can be said to typify the cooking of this region: prosciutto and parmesan cheese. For an extra special dish, sprinkle shavings of raw white truffle on top of the melted cheese just before serving.

Brodetto dell'Adriatico

Adriatic seafood soup

Serves: 6
Preparation: 30 minutes
Cooking: 1 hour
Recipe grading: fairly easy

- 4 lb/2 kg assorted uncleaned fish or 3 lb/1.5 kg filleted fish (gray mullet, red mullet, large shrimp, eels, scorpion fish, squid, shark or dogfish)
- 1 onion, finely chopped
- 3 cloves garlic, peeled
- about ½ cup/125 ml olive oil
- scant 1 cup/200 ml sieved tomatoes/ passata
- 4 tablespoons wine vinegar
- 1 tablespoon finely chopped parsley
- salt and freshly ground black pepper
- 6 thick slices coarse white bread, toasted

Suggested wine: a dry red
(Bosco Eliceo Merlot)

Clean, then trim and draw (gut) all the fish, removing and discarding the gills, scales, and the interior quill of the squid. ▪ Cut the larger fish into thick slices. ▪ Sauté the onion and the whole garlic cloves in the oil. Discard the cloves once they start to color. ▪ Pour in the sieved tomatoes and the vinegar. Simmer uncovered for about 30 minutes to reduce. ▪ Add the fish gradually, beginning with the firmest types which need longer cooking (squid followed by scorpion fish, large shrimp, eel). Pour in sufficient water to cover the fish, then add the parsley, salt, and pepper. Cover and simmer gently for 30 minutes more. ▪ Place the toasted bread in individual heated bowls and ladle the fish soup onto it. ▪ Serve hot.

Typical of the entire Romagnol coast (each town having its own version), Brodetto originated as an improvised dish on fishermen's boats, made with the least valuable fish and leftover bread. Traditionally canned tomato purée, diluted when necessary, was used instead of fresh tomatoes, with some good wine vinegar. Usually served as a main course, it is substantial enough to be a meal in itself.

Arista alla reggiana
Roast pork Reggio-style

Serves: 4
Preparation: 15 minutes + 24 hours
to marinate
Cooking: 1 hour
Recipe grading: easy

- 3½ lb/1.5 kg loin of pork
- 1 cup/250 ml extra-virgin olive oil
- 2 tablespoons wine vinegar
- 2 cloves garlic, peeled and lightly crushed
- 1 sprig rosemary
- 6–7 juniper berries
- 4¼ cups/1 liter whole milk (or enough to cover the meat, see method)
- salt and freshly ground black pepper

Suggested wine: a lightly sparkling, medium or dry red (Colli Piacentini Bonarda)

Tie the meat up with kitchen string so that it will keep its shape as it cooks. ▪ Choose a non-metallic fireproof casserole just large enough to accommodate the meat. Pour in the oil and vinegar, then add the garlic, rosemary, juniper berries, and, finally, the meat. Leave to marinate for 24 hours, turning frequently. ▪ Pour in sufficient milk to cover the meat, season with salt and pepper, and cook over a low heat for 1 hour. At the end of this time the milk will have been completely absorbed. ▪ Turn up the heat and brown the meat all over. ▪ Serve, carving into chops, slicing between the ribs. ▪ This dish is also very good served cold.

A loin of pork, still on the bone, is known as Arista *in many regions of Italy.*

Cotolette alla parmigiana

Veal cutlets Parma-style

Beat the veal lightly with a meat bat (pounder) to flatten evenly. ▪ Lightly beat the egg and a dash of salt together, then dip the escalopes in the mixture. ▪ Heat the butter in a skillet (frying pan) and fry the cutlets until light golden brown all over. ▪ Arrange in a single layer in a fireproof casserole which has been greased with butter. Cover with a layer of the parmesan shavings. Add the hot stock, then cover and cook over a low heat until the cheese has melted. ▪ Serve very hot.

Serves: 4
Preparation: 15 minutes
Cooking: 25 minutes
Recipe grading: easy

- 4 veal escalopes
- 1 large egg
- dash of salt
- 6 tablespoons butter
- ¾ cup/90 g parmesan cheese, in small shavings
- ½ cup/125 ml hot meat stock (homemade or bouillon cube)

Suggested wine: a dry red
(Colli di Parma Rosso)

These tasty cutlets are very easy to prepare.

Valigini

Veal rolls

Melt half the butter and mix thoroughly with the parsley, garlic, bread crumbs, parmesan, eggs, salt, and pepper in a bowl. ▪ Spread this mixture on the meat slices and then roll each slice up, securing with kitchen thread or wooden sticks. ▪ Sauté the onion in the remaining butter in a large heavy-bottomed saucepan or skillet (frying pan). ▪ Add the sieved tomatoes, then season with salt and pepper. ▪ Place the veal rolls in the pan in a single layer. Cover and cook over a low heat for about 15 minutes, turning them now and then. ▪ Serve hot.

Serves: 6
Preparation: 20 minutes
Cooking: 15 minutes
Recipe grading: easy

- scant $\frac{1}{2}$ cup/100 g butter
- 1 tablespoon finely chopped parsley
- 1 clove garlic, finely chopped
- 1 cup/125 g fine dry bread crumbs
- 1$\frac{1}{4}$ cups/150 g freshly grated parmesan cheese
- 2 large eggs
- salt and freshly ground black pepper
- 1$\frac{1}{2}$ lb/750 g thinly sliced escalopes of veal
- 1 small onion, finely chopped
- 2 tablespoons sieved tomatoes/passata diluted with $\frac{1}{2}$ cup/125 ml water

Suggested wine: a dry white
(Colli di Parma Sauvignon)

Neat slices of veal cut from the fillet or taken from a boned leg of veal and trimmed to the same size are best for this specialty of Emilia Romagna. A very large slice of veal can be used to make a single roll, which will need to cook for about 30 minutes.

The wines of Emilia Romagna

In wine too, Emilia and Romagna have quite separate tastes and traditions. Emilia is the land of lightly sparkling reds—*Gutturnio*, *Bonarda*, and, above all, *Lambrusco*. Romagna is home to the white wines, *Trebbiano* and *Albana* and, most important of all, the red *Sangiovese*. Wine has been made in both areas since the earliest times. The Umbri and Liguri, prehistoric inhabitants of the area, both made wines, while the Etruscans (800–300 BC) are said to have invented *Lambrusco*. The Romans also made *Lambrusco* and Pliny the Elder praised its therapeutic properties. Noted for its well-rounded, satisfying taste, *Lambrusco* takes its name from the Modenese dialect in which *brusca* means "sharp" (or spontaneous and fresh). The poet Giosué Carducci was very fond of

Lambrusco and drank it with all sorts of food, as does many a foreigner, appreciating its light and lively character. Its cheerful and attractive personality has helped to make *Lambrusco* one of the most popular Italian wines abroad, as well as one of the most widely drunk in Italy itself. It has been described as "the boldest in the world, the most generous, the most liberated, and the most Italian of wines."

Lambrusco is made from Lambrusca grapes. It is a wine that should be drank young and this has, perhaps, prevented it from capturing an even wider market. There are several designated production zones, including Grasparossa di Castelvetro, Parma, Reggiano, Salamino di Santa Croce, and Sorbara. Usually dry or semi-sweet, these wines are a very intense, almost purple color with a lively, evanescent froth and a winey scent with a pronounced bouquet. Lambrusco goes down very well with typical Emilian dishes, especially with appetizers of cured meats, Tortellini al ragù (stuffed pasta with rich meat sauce), Zampone (stuffed pig's trotter), and with all pork dishes. It is reputed to aid digestion and lower cholesterol, which provides even greater incentive for both the locals and foreigners to imbibe.

Many Romagnols say that *Sangiovese* is mother's milk to them, something familiar which evokes childhood memories and time honored family traditions.

The origins of Romagna's premier white – *Albana* – are obscure, although some say that the Romans brought it with them from the Alban Hills (near Rome). Another white – *Trebbiano* – is Romagna's everyday wine. Light and breezy in taste, it goes particularly well with fish. Some very good red and white wines are made in the hills around Piacenza, to the north of Emilia Romagna. The Colli Piacentini area, once a part of Piedmont, produces red *Gutturnio*, *Barbera*, and *Pinot Nero*, as well as white *Trebbiano*, *Ortrugo*, *Pinot Grigio*, and *Sauvignon*.

Over one hundred *Sangiovese* wines are produced in many areas. The wine's name is derived from Sanguis Jovis or "Blood of Jupiter," in reference to the pagan god who is said to have taught humans to love the land and each other. *Sangiovese* qualifies as Riserva after it has been aged for two years, and Superiore if it comes from one of the classic production zones. It can be aged for up to nine years. Aged *Sangiovese* goes well with rich meat sauces, croquettes, roast meat, and game. With its full body, ample flavor, and deep ruby red color, often with a hint of violet, good *Sangiovese* can be an exciting wine. At its best it is elegant, complex, well structured, full bodied and harmonious. *Sangiovese* novello also deserves a mention: this new season's wine is fragrant, dry, fresh and full of gaiety, but not excessively so. I well remember a nice old man who was a hearty drinker and who declared himself to be a devout disciple of the patron saint of all wine lovers: San Giovese!

Serves: 6
Preparation: 20 minutes
Cooking: 1 hour
Recipe grading: easy

- An oven-ready chicken weighing about 3½ lb/1.5 kg
- 1 medium onion, thinly sliced
- ½ cup/125 ml olive oil
- ¾ cup/90 g finely chopped fresh pork fat or pancetta or fat bacon
- 1 cup/250 ml dry white wine
- 8 oz/250 g ripe tomatoes, blanched, peeled and diced
- salt and freshly ground black pepper

Suggested wine: a dry white
(Colli Piacentini Malvasia Secco)

Pollo alla cacciatora

Hunter's chicken

Rinse the chicken inside and out under cold running water. Cut it into 8–12 small pieces, leaving it on the bone. Pat dry with paper towels. ▪ Sauté the onion in the oil until it colors. Then remove the onion from the pan and set aside. ▪ Add the pork fat or pancetta to the flavored oil, followed by the chicken pieces. Cook over a slightly higher heat for about 10 minutes, turning frequently. ▪ Pour in the wine and cook until it evaporates. ▪ Add the tomatoes and the reserved onion. Season with salt and pepper. ▪ Continue cooking for about 30 minutes, stirring and turning at intervals. ▪ Serve very hot.

This appetizing dish symbolizes convivial get-togethers and harvest feasts. In Parma and the surrounding area, chopped garlic, sage, and carrot are fried with the onion.

Fegato all'aceto balsamico

Calf's liver with balsamic vinegar

Coat the slices of liver with flour. Dip in the beaten egg and then coat with bread crumbs. Sprinkle lightly with salt and pepper. ▪ Heat the butter in a wide skillet (frying pan). Add the liver and cook until golden brown on both sides. ▪ Drain very briefly on paper towels to absorb excess fat. ▪ Drizzle with balsamic vinegar and serve at once.

Serves: 4
Preparation: 10 minutes
Cooking: 15 minutes
Recipe grading: easy

- 14 oz/400 g calf's liver, very thinly sliced
- ½ cup/75 g all-purpose/plain flour
- 2 large eggs, beaten
- scant 1 cup/100 g fine dry bread crumbs
- salt and freshly ground black pepper
- 4 tablespoons butter
- 2 tablespoons best-quality Modena balsamic vinegar

Suggested wine: a dry red
(Colli Piacentini Barbere Secco)

This dish has developed from a very old recipe and is well known in most areas of Emilia. Pig's liver can be used instead of calf's liver. In the older, original recipe, lard was used for frying instead of butter.

71

Cappone ripieno

Roast stuffed capon

Use a very sharp pointed knife to bone out the capon partially. Start with an incision down its backbone, gradually cutting the flesh away from the bones, taking great care not to puncture the skin. Carefully cut out and remove most of the breast meat and set aside, leaving only a thin layer attached to the skin. There is no need to remove the bones from the wings, thighs, and legs. Some butchers will do this boning for you. ▪ In a large mixing bowl, combine the veal, pork, mortadella, finely chopped hard-cooked eggs, the parmesan, Marsala, nutmeg, salt, and pepper. ▪ Cut the breast meat into short, thin strips. Stuff the boned capon with one-third of the mixture, spreading it inside the boned bird as evenly as possible. Then cover with a layer of one-third each of the strips of breast, ham, and prosciutto. Repeat this layering process twice. ▪ Sew the cut edges of the capon skin with kitchen thread, as neatly as possible, aiming to restore the capon almost to its original shape. Tie the legs and wings closely to the stuffed body with kitchen string and place in a large roasting pan. ▪ Season with salt and pepper, then sprinkle with the olive oil and dot the surface with small pieces of butter. ▪ Roast in a preheated oven at 400°F/200°C/gas 6 for about 2 hours, basting with its own cooking juices. ▪ Leave to stand and cool when done for 1 hour. Slice off the legs and wings. Cut the stuffed section into slices and arrange on a platter, sprinkled with the cooking juices. ▪ This partially boned capon is also delicious when cooked in a kettle or very large saucepan of gently simmering water, wrapped tightly in a clean white cloth or cheesecloth.

Serves: 6–8
Preparation: 1 hour
Cooking: 2 hours + time to rest
Recipe grading: complicated

- An oven-ready capon, weighing about 4 lb/2 kg
- 2 cups/250 g ground lean veal
- 2 cups/250 g ground lean pork
- 1 cup/150 g diced mortadella
- 4 hard-cooked eggs, finely chopped
- 1¼ cups/150 g freshly grated parmesan cheese
- 5 tablespoons dry Marsala wine
- dash of freshly grated nutmeg
- salt and freshly ground black pepper
- 5 oz/150 g lean ham, cut into thin strips
- 5 oz/150 g prosciutto/Parma ham, cut into thin strips
- ½ cup/125 ml olive oil
- 4 tablespoons butter, cut into small pieces

Suggested wine: a medium or dry red (Colli Piacentini Bonarda)

Capons are male chickens which are castrated when they are 2 months old. Great care is taken over their feed, which gives the meat an unmistakable flavor and texture. They are mainly eaten at Christmas time. Capons reared in Emilia are particularly sought-after.

Rifreddo

Chilled veal and ham mold

Serves: 6
Preparation: 20 minutes
Cooking: 2 hours + 2–3 hours' chilling
Recipe grading: fairly easy

- 4 escalopes of veal, each weighing about 5 oz/150 g
- 2 slices lean ham, each weighing about 5 oz/150 g
- 2 slices mortadella, each weighing about 5 oz/150 g
- freshly ground black pepper
- scant 1 cup/100 g freshly grated parmesan cheese
- 2 large eggs, beaten

Suggested wine: a dry red
(Colli Piacentini Pinot Nero)

Beat the veal slices lightly with a meat (pounder) bat to make them a little thinner and flatter. ▪ Trim them to size so that they will fit into a deep loaf pan about 8½ in/ 20–22 cm when laid out flat. Make sure that the ham and mortadella slices will also fit into it in the same way. ▪ Grease the loaf pan with butter. ▪ Layer the ingredients in the loaf pan, starting with a slice of veal in the bottom, followed by a slice of ham and then mortadella. Sprinkle each layer liberally with freshly ground pepper and parmesan cheese. ▪ Place another slice of veal on top. Pour the beaten eggs over it, then follow with another veal slice, the second ham slice, and the second slice of mortadella. Sprinkle each layer with pepper and parmesan. Finish with the last veal slice, pressing the layers down in the cake pan. ▪ Cover with aluminum foil and place the cake pan in a large roasting pan. Add enough boiling water to the roasting pan to come one-third of the way up the sides of the cake pan (or place in a steamer). Cook for 2 hours. ▪ When done, carefully pour off the cooking juices into a shallow, straight-sided dish. Turn the molded, layered meat out onto a serving dish and place a large, flat plate on top of it. Place a weight on the plate and leave to cool to room temperature. ▪ Chill the mold and its juices, separately, in the refrigerator for 2–3 hours. ▪ Serve, carved in thin, vertical slices. Garnish with the jellied cooking juices.

This dish is a specialty of Reggio Emilia.
A similar dish is made in Parma, where the
mortadella is replaced by prosciutto.

Cristoforo Messisbugo at the Court of the Dukes of Este in Ferrara

Cristoforo Messisbugo was of Flemish origin and lived at the court of the Dukes of Este in Ferrara, where he occupied the position of Knight Palatine in recognition of his talents as the *scalco*, or "Steward-Carver" (literally: a cutter and jointer of meat) and as a refined and eclectic gastronome. During the Renaissance era, the skills of Steward-Carvers were much in demand at the most fashionable European courts and members of the Italian school enjoyed a very high reputation. The post of Steward-Carver carried great prestige at court; medieval tradition had decreed that the Steward must be a nobleman capable of entertaining guests, as well as showing great faithfulness and loyalty to his lord and master: essential qualities at a time when enemies were often dispatched by means of poison!

The Renaissance banquet was a cultural event and symbolized a society which expressed itself through the art of display and a life lived according to ceremonial rules and customs.

Messisbugo's banquets were famous in the royal courts of Europe. They included quite lengthy intervals between courses during which guests could enjoy dancing, music, plays, singing, games, and conversation. Messisbugo's most famous banquet – the Dinner of Meat and Fish– was held at the court of Duke Ercole D'Este in 1529. The extravagant decorations included twenty-five painted statues made out of sugar which were placed along one table to illustrate the theme "The Labors of Hercules who slew the Lion," an allusion to his master, Duke Ercole (Hercules).

The appetizers (a choice of twenty-five) were placed on the tables.

They included slices of beef, ham, and tongue fried with sugar and cinnamon; a salad of capers, truffles, and seedless white raisins; soused porgy with bay leaves, and many more. The guests entered to a fanfare of trumpets and the banquet commenced. It progressed through eight multiple services or "removes" each consisting of several courses, mainly of meat, fish, and game; each remove comprised 10–12 courses. After the fifth remove the tables were cleared and relaid with a white bread roll for each guest. More allegorical figures made of sugar were carried in amid general applause. The last course was followed by sweetmeats, such as candied citron, quince cheese, and sugared almonds. Then the dancing began, continuing into the early hours of the next morning, with sugar, lettuce, watermelon, and other fruits served at 3 am.

In 1549, after Messisbugo's death, a book was published which not only contained over 300 recipes and information about food but also included what amounted to a treatise on contemporary Ferrarese usages and customs. Although known simply as The New Book, its full title was "The New Book, in which the Reader is instructed how to prepare every type of Food depending on the Season, whether it be Meat or Fish and the correct form for Banquets, laying tables, provisioning of Palaces and decorating rooms at any Princely court. A very fine work, of great use to Court Chamberlains, Steward-Carvers, Stewards of the Pantry, and Cooks."

The book is divided into three parts: an introduction about organizing banquets; a list of ten dinner menus, three luncheon menus and one for a banquet, all described in minute detail; and a recipe book with 315 recipes. In the introduction the author explains that he does not wish to describe simple and traditional local fare, but to confine himself to elaborate dishes belonging to what was then considered "haute cuisine." Not content with inventing totally new recipes, Messisbugo adapted and refined many popular dishes of the day. He also introduced some foreign recipes, having first modified them to appeal to local taste, an innovative step at the time.

Beef Stock
Makes about 2½ quarts/2.5 liters.

1 lb/500 g lean beef (brisket, rump, shank or shin)
½ chicken or capon
generous 3 quarts/3 liters cold water
1 stalk celery, washed and cut into pieces
1 carrot, peeled and cut into large pieces
1 onion, peeled
2 stalks parsley
1 small, ripe tomato
coarse sea salt to taste

Place the meat and poultry in a kettle or very large saucepan, cover with cold water, and bring to the boil. ▪ Skim off any scum (this is produced by the albumen on the surface of the meat which coagulates as it heats) and then add all the vegetables and seasonings. Add a generous dash of salt and simmer for about 2 hours. ▪ Strain before using.

Zampone con lenticchie
Stuffed pig's trotter with lentils

Place the zampone in a large bowl of cold water and leave to soak for 12 hours. ▪ In a separate bowl soak the lentils for 12 hours. ▪ Just before cooking the zampone, take it out of the water and use a large darning needle to prick the skin, puncturing it at intervals along its length, making 2 or 3 lines of holes. Use the tip of a very sharp, pointed knife to make a small cross-cut incision on the underside of the trotter (between the three toes). Slightly loosen the string used to tie it up. These three precautions will prevent it bursting as it cooks. ▪ Wrap the zampone in a piece of cheesecloth (or a clean white cloth) and place in a large saucepan or kettle. Cover completely with cold water and simmer very gently for 3–4 hours. ▪ While the zampone is cooking, prepare the lentils: sauté the pancetta for a few minutes in the oil, then add the onion. ▪ When the onion has softened, add the lentils and stir while cooking for a few minutes. ▪ Add sufficient boiling water to cover the lentils completely and crumble the bouillon cube into the water. ▪ Simmer gently over a low heat for 1½ hours. ▪ Unwrap the zampone and serve very hot, cut into ¼ in/5 mm slices, accompanied by the lentils.

Serves: 4–6
Preparation: 20 minutes + 12 hours' soaking
Cooking: 3–4 hours for the zampone,
1½ hours for the lentils
Recipe grading: easy

- 1 zampone (stuffed pig's foot/trotter) weighing about 2 lb/1 kg
- 1½ cups/300 g lentils (small brown or Puy type)
- ¾ cup/90 g finely chopped pancetta
- 2 tablespoons olive oil
- 1 medium onion, finely chopped
- boiling water
- 1 stock/bouillon cube

Suggested wine: a dry red
(Colli Piacentini Gutturnio)

This tasty pork product is another specialty from Modena. It consists of a pig's forefoot stuffed with a mixture of meat, pork skin, and seasonings. Traditional Modena pig's foot/trotter needs very lengthy cooking, but good quality pre-cooked zamponi are available from stores specializing in Italian foods. When served with lentils it is this region's traditional New Year's dish, symbolizing prosperity and good fortune.

The French cooks at the court of Duchess Marie Louise of Parma introduced the custom of serving a very alcoholic zabaglione with this dish, made with white wine and a dash of cognac. For another very tasty sauce, combine 1¼ cups/150 g freshly grated parmesan cheese with 5 tablespoons of Modena's famous balsamic vinegar.

Fritto alla Garisenda

Fried eggy bread with cheese and prosciutto

Cut the crusts off the bread. ▪ Then use a pastry cutter or the rim of a small glass to cut out disks of about 2 in/5 cm in diameter. ▪ Make sandwiches with pairs of these disks, placing between them a slice of prosciutto and of cheese (trimmed to a slightly smaller size than the bread disks). ▪ If you are using truffle, place shavings of it between the meat and cheese layers. ▪ Press the layers to make them stick together. ▪ Dip them very quickly in the cold milk, then in the beaten eggs, and finally coat with bread crumbs. Dip the sandwiches into the egg again, and finish with another coating of bread crumbs. ▪ Check that the edges of the sandwiches stay firmly stuck together and are well coated with egg and bread crumbs. Otherwise the filling will ooze out when they are fried, as the cheese melts. ▪ Heat the butter in a wide skillet (frying pan) and fry the sandwiches, turning once, until they are golden brown. ▪ Drain on paper towels and serve piping hot.

Serves: 6
Preparation: 25 minutes
Cooking: 20 minutes
Recipe grading: fairly easy

- 24 slices from a white loaf (slightly stale)
- 4 oz/125 g prosciutto/Parma ham, thinly sliced
- 5 oz/150 g parmesan or gruyère cheese, sliced
- 1 white truffle (optional)
- ½ cup/125 ml milk
- 3 large eggs
- 1¼ cups/150 g fine dry bread crumbs
- 7 tablespoons butter

Suggested wine: a lightly sparkling, dry red (Lambrusco di Sorbara)

Named after one of Bologna's historic towers, this appetizing fried dish also makes an excellent snack.

Serves: 4
Preparation: 25 minutes
Cooking: about 1½ hours
Recipe grading: easy

- 1 large, thin slice from rump of beef weighing about 8 oz/250 g
- 1 cotechino sausage, weighing about 10 oz/300 g
- 1 small onion, coarsely chopped
- 1 stalk celery, coarsely chopped
- 1 small carrot, coarsely chopped
- 2 tablespoons butter
- ½ cup/125 ml dry red wine
- 2 oz/60 g dried Italian mushrooms, soaked in warm water, drained, and chopped
- 2 cups/500 ml water

Suggested wine: a dry red
(Colli Piacentini Gutturnio)

Cotechino in galera
Cotechino sausage with beef and vegetables

Use a meat (pounder) bat to flatten the slice of beef. ▪ Skin the cotechino sausage. Wrap it up in the slice of beef, enveloping it completely. Tie the resulting roll securely but not too tightly with kitchen string. ▪ Sauté the onion, celery, and carrot in the butter for a few minutes. ▪ Add the meat and sausage roll, and brown well all over. ▪ Pour in the wine and cook until it has evaporated. ▪ Add the mushrooms and the water they were soaked in. ▪ Simmer gently for 1½ hours. ▪ Untie the string and serve. Slice, moistening with the cooking juices.

As Artusi said, this may not be a refined recipe, "but as a family dish it is very good indeed, and you can even serve it to your friends with confidence." It certainly makes a very flavorsome, robust, and nourishing meal.

Anguilla all'uso di Comacchio

Stewed eel Comacchio-style

Skin the eels. Cut off its head and then draw (gut) it. ▪ Sauté the onions and garlic in the oil until they have softened a little. ▪ Add the vinegar, followed by the tomato paste diluted with water. Season with salt and pepper. Add the eel and cook over a low heat for 30 minutes. Do not stir the eel while it cooks as the flesh breaks up very easily—simply shake the pan from side to side now and then to prevent it sticking. ▪ Serve very hot.

Serves: 4
Preparation: 20 minutes
Cooking: 35 minutes
Recipe grading: easy

- 2 lb/1 kg eels
- 2 large onions, finely chopped
- 1 clove garlic, finely chopped
- 2 tablespoons extra-virgin olive oil
- 2 tablespoons good wine vinegar
- 2 tablespoons tomato paste, diluted in 1 cup/250 ml water
- salt and freshly ground black pepper

Suggested wine: a dry red
(Sangiovese di Romagna)

Eels are very slippery creatures and difficult to handle. Ask your supplier to skin the eel and cut its head off for you. If you must do it yourself, rub wood ash or coarse salt all over the skin to make it easier to hold. This traditional dish is from Comacchio, a coastal area of Romagna, where eels have been farmed in lagoons from time immemorial. Eels spend most of their lives in fresh water, although they breed at sea. Most eels are caught from October to December as they leave the rivers on their way to the open sea or when the elvers return several months later.

Parma ham and other cured meats

Parma ham, or *prosciutto crudo di Parma*, as it is known in Italy, is one of the prime delicacies of Italian cuisine and is known throughout the world. It takes its Italian name from the verb *prosciugare*, which means "to dry," combined with *crudo*, which means "raw." And in fact, it isn't cooked (unlike many of the imitations that are now made around the world), but is cured using salt, fresh air, and the skills accumulated during more than 2,000 years of practice. As early as

Homer's times (at least 800 BC), meats were preserved using salt, smoke, and air. These methods have remained unchanged through the ages and are still used to make this special ham. In Italy Parma ham is usually served as an appetizer. It is best with fresh cantaloupe (rock melon) or figs, which enhance its inimitable flavor, or with other cured meats. In Emilia Romagna it is often served with fried tidbits (such as *Crescenti*, see recipe, page 18), for a really naughty treat.

The pigs reared to make Parma ham are an Anglo-Danish crossbreed. They are fed on barley, oats, and soya flour for about a year until their legs have reached the required size. The fresh hams are cleaned, salted with just enough salt to draw out the moisture and preserve the meat, then stored for a few weeks in a cool, well-aired place. Finally they are washed again and aged for 10–12 months more. The ageing period depends on the size of the hams, which lose a considerable amount of their weight during this process. By law, the seal of the Duchy of Parma must be stamped on each ham.

One of the most highly prized and expensive of all Italian cured meats is made in the area around the little town of Zibello, in the province of Parma. Known as *Culatello*, it is made from the lower part of the hog's leg, which is boned, seasoned with salt, garlic, pepper, and other spices, and then folded and sewn into its own skin. Thinly sliced, it is served in all of the best restaurants in the region as an appetizer.

Many different types of salami are produced in Emilia Romagna, each with their own special mix of spices and ageing process. Bolognese salami is intensely perfumed and relatively soft, since it is only aged for about 4 months. *Salame di Felino* (right), made near Parma, arguably the best salami made in the region, has a much milder taste, but is aged for almost a year.

Mortadella is a specialty of the regional capital of Bologna, where it has been made for at least 600 years. This delicious buttery soft sausage is made from a special blend of finely minced pork, salt, and spices which are steamed very, very slowly, sometimes for up to 20 hours. The largest (and best) mortadella sausages are huge, weighing up to 200 pounds (100 kilos) or more and measuring 15 inches (40 cm) in diameter.

Canocchie ripiene

Stuffed broiled shrimp

Serves: 4–6
Preparation: 20 minutes
Cooking: 15 minutes
Recipe grading: easy

- 2 lb/1 kg jumbo shrimp
- 5 tablespoons fine dry bread crumbs
  (not toasted)
- 2 cloves garlic, finely chopped
- 1 tablespoon finely chopped parsley
- 2 tablespoons dry white wine
- 5 tablespoons extra-virgin olive oil
- salt and freshly ground black pepper

Suggested wine: a dry, fruity white
(Colli Piacentini Ortrugo)

Trim off the shrimp's legs and the protruding parts of the shell and eyes with sharp, pointed kitchen scissors. ▪ Use the scissors or a very sharp, pointed knife to cut their shells open down the center of their backs, without slicing the flesh beneath. ▪ Mix the bread crumbs with the garlic, parsley, wine, 2 tablespoons of the olive oil, salt, and pepper in a bowl. ▪ Stuff some of this mixture into the opening in the shell of each shrimp and brush the remaining oil all over the top. ▪ Arrange the shrimp in a single layer in a broiler pan (grill pan) and broil, turning once. Alternatively, place in a roasting pan (tin) and cook in a preheated oven at 400°F/200°C/gas 6 for 15 minutes.

*The original Italian
recipe calls for mantis
shrimp which live under the surface of
the sandy sea bed in the Adriatic Sea. They are
caught in large numbers with drag nets,
especially in the cold winter months.*

Rossal

Braised red mullet

Sauté the garlic with the parsley in the extra-virgin olive oil in a wide skillet (frying pan) or heavy-bottomed saucepan for 2–3 minutes. ▪ Add the tomatoes and season with salt and pepper. Simmer, uncovered, for 15 minutes to allow the sauce to reduce. ▪ Prepare the fish (trim them, then remove their heads and gut them). Coat with flour. ▪ Fry in very hot oil until they are pale golden brown. Drain on paper towels. ▪ Add the cooked red mullet to the sauce. Let them absorb its flavor for a few minutes and then serve.

Rossal is the Romagnol dialect name for young mullet which are caught in September along the Adriatic coast. These fish are very small, not more than 2¹⁄₂ in/6–7 cm in length, and very tender. Red mullet are delicate, breaking up easily even when raw; they need careful handling and shorter cooking times than other fish. For a lighter dish, omit the frying stage and cook the fish gently in the sauce.

Serves: 4
Preparation: 20 minutes
Cooking: 30 minutes
Recipe grading: easy

- 1 clove garlic, whole
- 2 tablespoons finely chopped parsley
- ¹⁄₂ cup/125 ml extra-virgin olive oil
- 12 oz/350 g ripe tomatoes, blanched, peeled, and coarsely chopped
- 1 lb/500 g cleaned young red mullet
- salt and freshly ground black pepper
- ³⁄₄ cup/125 g all-purpose/plain flour
- olive oil, for frying

Suggested wine: a dry, fruity white (Colli di Parma Sauvignon)

Verdure

Endive with pancetta and balsamic vinegar	89
Stuffed zucchini	90
Cheese and potato pie	94
Marinated eggplants	95
Fried pumpkin	96
Asparagus with parmesan cheese	98
Savory onions and tomatoes	99

The fertile plains of Emilia Romagna are ideal for growing fruit and vegetables. Every year, farmers in the region harvest abundant crops of tomatoes, zucchini (courgettes), eggplants (aubergines), fennel, pumpkin, asparagus, and a host of other quality produce. These vegetables have found their way into a variety of dishes, from the sweet pumpkin-filled pasta of Ferrara, to the typical spinach pasta used in Bolognese lasagna. In this chapter we look at some of the traditional recipes that can be served as side dishes.

Radicchio all'aceto balsamico

Endive with pancetta and balsamic vinegar

Rinse and dry the endives. Separate the leaves and arrange them in a ceramic or heatproof bowl. ▪ Sauté the pancetta and garlic in the butter until it is light golden brown. ▪ Add the balsamic vinegar and a dash of salt then remove from the heat. ▪ Pour over the endives and serve immediately before the salad greens start to wilt.

Serves: 6
Preparation: 15 minutes
Cooking: 10 minutes
Recipe grading: easy

- ▪ 1 lb/500 g Red Treviso endive or Belgian endive/chicory
- ▪ 1 cup/120 g finely diced pancetta or fat bacon
- ▪ 2 cloves garlic, finely chopped
- ▪ 2 tablespoons butter
- ▪ 2 tablespoons best-quality Modena balsamic vinegar
- ▪ dash of salt

Suggested wine: a lightly sparkling, dry white (Colli Piacentini Malvasia)

This delicious warm salad is locally known as pote *and is the ideal accompaniment to roast meat and poultry, fried dishes, and veal escalopes.*

Serves: 4
Preparation: 20 minutes
Cooking: 30 minutes
Recipe grading: easy

- 4 long zucchini/courgettes
- 1 tablespoon finely chopped parsley
- 1 clove garlic, finely chopped
- ½ cup/60 g fine dry bread crumbs
- ½ cup/60 g freshly grated parmesan cheese
- 1 large egg
- 2 tablespoons milk
- 1 large scallion/spring onion, thinly sliced
- 4 tablespoons butter
- 2 tablespoons sieved tomatoes/passata
- salt and freshly ground black pepper

Suggested wine: a lightly sparkling, dry white (Colli Bolognesi Bianco Asciutto Vivace)

Zucchine ripiene

Stuffed zucchini

Wash the zucchini. Trim off the ends and cut lengthwise in half. ▪ Use a melon baller to scoop out the center of the zucchini. Chop the flesh finely, then mix it with the parsley, garlic, bread crumbs, parmesan, egg, and milk in a bowl. ▪ Fill the hollowed-out zucchini with this mixture. ▪ Sauté the scallion in the butter in a very wide skillet (frying pan) until tender. Add the sieved tomatoes and season with salt and pepper. ▪ Arrange the zucchini in a single layer in the skillet with the tomato mixture. Pour in sufficient water to come halfway up their sides. ▪ Cook over a moderate heat for 20 minutes. ▪ Serve warm.

An alternative, meat-based version of this dish can be prepared as follows: sauté 1 stalk celery, 1 onion, and 1 carrot, all finely chopped, in the butter with 2½ cups/300 g finely ground lean beef. Cook for 15 minutes, stirring frequently. Combine the meat mixture with the same ingredients as the recipe above, omitting the garlic. Fill the zucchini with this mixture and cook as explained above.

Balsamic vinegar – black gold

Balsamic vinegar is produced in the Emilian town of Modena. It is made with the unfermented grape juice or "must" from carefully selected Trebbiano grapes, which undergo a very lengthy process before they become the dark, flavorsome elixir used to season meats, salads, and vegetables. After being transferred from one barrel to another once a year for five years, a quintal (220 lb/100 kg) of grape must yields approximately 2 quarts (2 liters) of balsamic vinegar. The time, patience, and skill required to produce balsamic vinegar make the top quality brands very expensive. One-hundred-year-old balsamic vinegar, aged in oak or juniper wood casks, can cost up to one million Italian lire per liter, which is the equivalent of around $650 for one quart! However, for real connoisseurs no price is too high to pay for this extraordinary glowing liquid, with its pronounced yet subtle aroma and thick, almost syrupy consistency. Its bittersweet taste enhances ices, strawberries, boiled and roast meats, salads, and frittatas. Now that balsamic vinegar has become so widely known, a consortium has been set up to safeguard its quality and to protect the consumer from the many improbably cheap and inferior imitations.

Woodland salad with balsamic vinegar
Serves 4

¾ cup/150 g whole grain/brown rice
½ cup/100 g wild black or red rice
12 cups/500 g mixed wild salad greens
2 cups/300 g fresh raspberries
1 bunch arugula/rocket, cut fine with scissors
1 bunch salad burnet or pimpinella leaves
15 leaves fresh mint
1 bunch fresh chervil, in sprigs
2 bunches cress, coarsely chopped
4 carrots, finely grated
4 tablespoons extra-virgin olive oil
4–6 tablespoons best quality balsamic vinegar

Cook the rice in salted, boiling water until tender. ▪ Wash and dry the mixed salad greens. Place in a large salad bowl, add the herbs, and toss well. ▪ Sprinkle with the carrot and garnish with almost all the raspberries. ▪ Drain the rice and transfer to a bowl. Add the oil. ▪ Place in a large serving dish and garnish with the remaining raspberries. ▪ Drizzle with the balsamic vinegar and serve.

To make the vinegar, the must is filtered, then boiled until it has reduced to one-third of its original volume. It is then cooled and poured into a large barrel, usually of oak, where it remains for at least one year. Each year thereafter the vinegar is transferred to barrels of diminishing size made of different woods, in the following order: chestnut, cherry, ash, and mulberry. It is in these wood-scented barrels that the vinegar acquires its distinctive taste, body, and color.

Each year some boiled, concentrated grape must is added, to replace the volume of must lost, partly through evaporation and partly as a result of the fermentation process. The original liquid undergoes a very slow transformation, becoming more and more concentrated. Balsamic vinegar is always matured in cool, well ventilated places.

The adjective "balsamic" denotes the vinegar's medicinal properties (which it shares with ordinary vinegars). Hippocrates, the most famous physician of the ancient world, prescribed the application of bandages soaked in vinegar to heal sores and wounds, and extolled its therapeutic value for curing illnesses of the respiratory tract. Vinegar was later used as a disinfectant for people and objects during epidemics of plague and smallpox, while in the nineteenth century it was used to revive delicate young ladies when they fell swooning onto chaise longues and sofas.

Balsamic vinegar's origins are extremely ancient and the Romans apparently knew how to make it. The process was turned into an art at the court of the Dukes of Este, where the secrets of its preparation were as mysterious as its taste was famous. The art of producing balsamic vinegar was handed down among the oldest families of Modena until fairly recent times. Barrels of balsamic vinegar were left by grandparents to their grandchildren in their wills, or were given as family wedding presents.

Tortino di patate

Cheese and potato pie

Serves: 4
Preparation: 20 minutes
Cooking: 45 minutes
Recipe grading: easy

- 1½ lb/750 g firm, waxy potatoes
- ½ cup/125 g butter
- 8 oz/250 g piece parmesan cheese, rind removed
- salt and freshly ground black pepper
- 1 cup/250 ml milk

Suggested wine: a lightly sparkling, dry red (Colli Piacentini Gutturnio Secco Vivace)

Wash the potatoes thoroughly. Boil them with their skins on for about 20 minutes, or until tender but still firm. ▪ Peel while hot and set aside to cool. ▪ Cut into ½ in/1 cm slices and arrange in layers in a deep ovenproof dish greased with butter. Distribute flakes of butter and thin slices of the parmesan over each layer, then sprinkle with salt and pepper. ▪ Pour in the milk and bake in a preheated oven at 400°F/200°C/gas 6 for 25 minutes.

This simple, inexpensive dish goes very well with roast meat and poultry. For extra flavor, add a little grated nutmeg.

Melanzane marinate

Marinated eggplants

Trim, then wash and dry the eggplants. Slice them thinly lengthwise and arrange in layers in a colander, sprinkling each layer liberally with salt. Cover with a suitably sized plate. Place a weight on top and set aside for 1 hour. The eggplants will release their bitter liquid and will absorb less oil as they cook. ▪ Dry the degorged eggplants thoroughly with paper towels. ▪ Heat sufficient oil to shallow fry them in a large skillet or frying pan (preferably made of cast iron). ▪ Cook until golden brown and drain on paper towels. ▪ Arrange in layers in a deep, straight sided-dish, placing slices of garlic and sage leaves between the layers. ▪ Pour in sufficient wine vinegar to completely cover the top layer. Leave to stand for 24 hours before serving.

Serves: 6
Preparation: 20 minutes + 1 hour to degorge the eggplants and 24 hours to marinate
Cooking: 20 minutes
Recipe grading: easy

- 4 fairly large eggplants/aubergines
- salt
- olive oil, for frying
- 2 cloves garlic, thinly sliced
- 8–10 leaves fresh sage
- good-quality wine vinegar (see method for quantity)

Suggested wine: a light, dry red
(Lambrusco Grasparossa)

This dish makes a tasty appetizer. It is also very good served with boiled meats or fish. Bay leaves can be used instead of sage leaves. Traditionally, lard (rendered fresh pork fat) was used to fry the eggplants.

Zucca fritta

Fried pumpkin

Serves: 4
Preparation: 10 minutes
Cooking: 15 minutes
Recipe grading: easy

- 2 lb/1 kg piece of yellow pumpkin
- ¾ cup/125 g all-purpose/plain flour
- oil, for frying (olive or sunflower)
- salt

Suggested wine: a light, dry white
(Colli Piacentini Pinot Grigio)

Peel the pumpkin. Remove the seeds and the fibrous layer beneath them. Cut the flesh into slices ½ in/1 cm thick and 1½ in/4 cm long. ▪ Coat lightly with flour, shaking off any excess. ▪ Heat plenty of oil in a skillet or frying pan until it is very hot. Fry the pumpkin pieces a few at a time until deep golden brown. ▪ Drain on paper towels. ▪ Sprinkle with a little salt and serve piping hot. ▪ For deliciously crisp pumpkin pieces, use a small saucepan and have the oil deep and very hot. Fry just a few pieces at a time, so that the temperature of the oil stays high. In this way the fried pieces will be lighter and contain less fat, since the very quick frying seals the vegetable immediately, and it absorbs less oil.

If you can't eat fried foods, try the following: preheat the oven to 400°F/200°C/gas 6. Spread the pumpkin pieces, cut ½ in/1 cm thick, out on a rack to bake. ▪ After 15 minutes increase the temperature to 425°F/220°C/gas 7 and cook for another 5 minutes. The pumpkin should be lightly browned. ▪ Serve hot with small pieces of butter and a sprinkling of salt and freshly ground pepper.

Pumpkin used to be an everyday food. There were even traveling street vendors who sold their hot fragrant baked pumpkin to passers-by. Nowadays consumption is mainly limited to certain regions, Emilia Romagna being one of them, where yellow pumpkins are still widely used in fillings and soups.

Serves: 6
Preparation: 20 minutes
Cooking: 30 minutes
Recipe grading: easy

- 4 lb/2 kg green asparagus
- ⅔ cup/150 g butter
- 1¼ cups/150 g freshly grated
  parmesan cheese
- salt

Suggested wine: a dry white
(Colli di Parma Sauvignon)

Asparagi alla parmigiana
Asparagus with parmesan cheese

Clean the asparagus thoroughly. Cut off the lower, tougher parts of the stalks and trim them all to the same length. ▪ Starting halfway up the green stalks, use a sharp knife to scrape off the thin outer skin from the lower half of each stalk. ▪ Rinse the asparagus in cold water, then tie up in one or more bundles with kitchen string. ▪ Place them upright, tips uppermost, in a deep, narrow saucepan. Pour in sufficient boiling water to come two-thirds of the way up the stalks, leaving the very tender tips out of the water so that they steam-cook, preserving even more of their delicate flavor. Cook for 10–20 minutes (depending on the thickness of the stalks), until tender. ▪ Use two forks to hook the string and lift the bundle(s) out of the boiling water. ▪ Leave to drain, then arrange in layers in an ovenproof dish greased with butter. Distribute flakes of butter and some of the parmesan on each layer, including the top one. Sprinkle lightly with salt. ▪ Cook in a preheated oven at 400°F/200°C/gas 6 for 10 minutes, or until the cheese has melted. ▪ Serve hot.

Asparagus is grown on a very large scale in Emilia Romagna, where it is highly prized for its delicate, slightly bitter taste.

Frizon

Savory onions and tomatoes

Sauté the onions in the oil in a large, heavy-bottomed saucepan until they are golden brown. ▪ Add the bell peppers and cook for 10 minutes more. ▪ Roughly chop the tomatoes and add to the pan. Season with salt and pepper. Simmer over a low heat for 30 minutes, stirring now and then. ▪ Serve hot or at room temperature.

Serves: 6
Preparation: 15 minutes
Cooking: 45 minutes
Recipe grading: easy

- 2 lb/1 kg onions, peeled and sliced
- 1 cup/250 ml extra-virgin olive oil
- 1 red bell pepper/capsicum and 1 yellow bell pepper, trimmed and cut into small pieces
- 1¼ lb/625 g ripe tomatoes, blanched and peeled
- salt and freshly ground black pepper

Suggested wine: a light, dry white (Colli Piacentini Trebbiano Val Trebbia)

A popular recipe for a vegetable dish-cum-sauce in which various leftovers are usually reheated. A Romagnol variation of this recipe includes 3 cups/750 g of fresh Italian sausage meat to be added before the tomatoes and sautéed with the onions and peppers. Some cooks also add diced yellow, waxy potatoes.

Dolci

Emilian trifle	101
Modena cake	103
Jam-filled turnovers	104
Brandy-flavored fritters	105
Amaretti and chocolate cake	106
Christmas pie	108
Cornmeal, pine nut, and raisin cookies	112
Rice cake	113
Black pie	115
Rice pudding Artusi-style	116

Delicious desserts, cakes, and cookies are served in Emilia Romagna to finish special family meals and to celebrate religious festivals. Brandy-flavored fritters and Jam-filled turnovers, for example, are served during Carnivale, the period leading up to Lent. Many dishes are linked to a particular town or village, where they were invented or adapted from traditional recipes to commemorate important events in local history. Some of the recipes in this chapter have been served for centuries.

Zuppa all'emiliana

Emilian trifle

Beat the sugar and egg yolks in a heatproof bowl until they are almost white. ▪ Stir in the flour, adding a little at a time to prevent lumps forming. ▪ Pour in the milk, stirring all the time. ▪ Place the bowl over a saucepan of gently simmering water. Cook, while stirring, until the mixture begins to thicken. ▪ Remove from the heat and pour half the custard into another bowl. ▪ Add the grated chocolate to the custard remaining in the first bowl. Replace over the simmering water until the chocolate has melted. Remove from the heat. ▪ Lightly grease a springform cake pan. ▪ Line the bottom with thin slices of sponge cake. Dip a pastry brush in the liqueur or rum and moisten the cake. ▪ When the plain custard has cooled, spread it over the cake. Cover with a layer of the jam, followed by the chocolate custard. Cover with a final layer of sponge cake, briefly dipped in the liqueur or rum. Chill in the refrigerator for 3–4 hours. Turn out onto a plate just before serving.

Serves: 4
Preparation: 45 minutes + 3–4 hours' chilling
Cooking: 15 minutes
Recipe grading: easy

- scant ½ cup/90 g superfine/caster sugar
- 3 large egg yolks
- ½ cup/75 g all-purpose/plain flour
- 3½ cups/800 ml warm milk
- 5 oz/150 g good-quality semisweet/dark chocolate, grated
- 1 sponge cake, weighing about 12 oz/350 g
- Alchermes or Maraschino liqueur or Jamaica rum
- generous ¾ cup/200 g Morello cherry or plum jam

Suggested wine: a sweet white (Albana Dolce)

This was traditionally served at country weddings and festivals. It resembles the Zuppa Inglese, *which is popular throughout Italy, but differs in the use of jam.*

Bensone

Modena cake

Sift the flour into a mixing bowl. ▪ Mix in the sugar, salt, lemon zest (yellow part only, without any of the white pith), and baking powder. ▪ Turn out onto a pastry board and heap up into a mound. Make a well in the center and add the butter and eggs (reserving 1 tablespoon of beaten egg to glaze the cake). ▪ Work these ingredients together, gradually combining them with the flour, and adding 2–3 tablespoons of milk. Knead the dough only just long enough to make it smooth and homogenous. ▪ Grease a baking sheet and dust with flour. ▪ Shape the dough into a long, thick sausage and place this in an S-shape on the baking sheet. ▪ Brush the surface with the reserved egg and sprinkle with the roughly crushed sugar. Using a sharp, pointed knife, make an incision along the center of the entire length of the cake. ▪ Bake in a preheated oven at 350°F/180°C/gas 4 for 40 minutes. ▪ Leave to cool on a cake rack for 10 minutes before serving.

Serves: 6
Preparation: 25 minutes
Cooking: 40 minutes
Recipe grading: easy

- 3⅓ cups/500 g all-purpose/plain flour
- ¾ cup/150 g superfine/caster sugar
- dash of salt
- finely grated zest of 1 lemon
- 3½ teaspoons baking powder
- ½ cup/125 g butter, chopped in small pieces
- 3 large eggs, lightly beaten
- 2–3 tablespoons milk
- scant ½ cup/90 g roughly crushed sugar (grains/crystals/nibs)

Suggested wine: a semisweet, lightly sparkling red
(Lambrusco di Sorbara Amabile)

In Modena this cake is usually served at the end of the meal, when it is dipped into the Lambrusco wine left in the diners' glasses. The recipe is very old indeed: it is known to have been made in Modena since 1300. It was usually baked on December 1 and given to the city's silversmiths and goldsmiths, whose patronal festival fell on that day. The Italian name Bensone *may be derived from a corruption of the old French* pain de benisson, *literally, "bread of blessing."*

Serves: 8
Preparation: 1 hour + 1 hour's resting
Cooking: 30 minutes
Recipe grading: fairly easy

- 3⅓ cups/500 g all-purpose/plain flour
- 1¼ cups/250 g superfine/caster sugar
- dash of salt
- ⅔ cup/150 g butter, cut into small pieces
- 3 large eggs
- 3 tablespoons Sassolino liqueur or Jamaica rum
- 1 tablespoon baking powder
- 1½ cups/400 g Morello cherry or plum jam
- confectioners'/icing sugar

Suggested wine: a medium sparkling white (Malvasia Rinaldini Amabile)

Tortelli di marmellata
Jam-filled turnovers

Mix the flour with the sugar and salt in a mixing bowl. Turn out onto a pastry board and heap up into a mound. ▪ Make a well in the center and add the butter, eggs, and liqueur or rum. Combine all these ingredients without working the dough too much, just enough to ensure it is smooth and homogenous. ▪ Shape into a ball, then cover with plastic wrap (cling film) and leave to rest for 1 hour. ▪ Roll the dough out into a sheet just under ¼ in/5 mm thick. Use a pastry cutter to cut out 3 in/7–8 cm diameter disks. ▪ Place a teaspoon of jam in the center of each disk and fold the disk in half to form a half-moon shape, enclosing the jam. Press the edges together to seal. ▪ Grease one or more baking sheets and dust with flour. Place the filled turnovers on the sheet(s), leaving plenty of space between them. ▪ Bake in a preheated oven at 375°F/190°C/gas 5 for 30 minutes. ▪ Leave to cool and dust with the confectioners' sugar.

These are usually associated with Carnival time, but they also make perfect treats for a child's birthday party or to serve with tea or coffee.

Sfrappole

Brandy-flavored fritters

Serves: 8
Preparation: 20 minutes + 2 hours' resting
Cooking: 15 minutes
Recipe grading: easy

Sift the flour into a mixing bowl and mix well with the sugar and salt. ▪ Turn out onto a pastry board and shape into a mound. Make a well in the center and add the butter, eggs, and brandy (or white wine with lemon zest). Combine all the ingredients, gradually working in the flour to form a smooth, well-blended dough. ▪ Cover with a clean cloth and leave to rest in a warm place for 2 hours. ▪ Roll out the dough to make a very thin sheet (just under ⅛ in/3 mm). ▪ Use a fluted pastry wheel to cut the pastry into strips 1¼ in/3 cm wide and 8 in/20 cm long. ▪ Tie each strip loosely into a knot and deep fry a few at a time in very hot oil until pale golden brown. ▪ Drain on paper towels. ▪ Dust lightly with the confectioners' sugar before serving.

- 3⅓ cups/500 g all-purpose/plain flour
- 2 tablespoons superfine/caster sugar
- dash of salt
- 2 tablespoons butter, cut into small pieces
- 4 large eggs
- 3 tablespoons Cognac (or other grape brandy) or white wine with finely grated lemon zest
- oil, for frying
- confectioners'/icing sugar

Suggested wine: a medium or dry sparkling white (Colli Bolognesi Pignoletto Amabile or Asciutto)

These are traditional carnival fare and are made all over Italy, under different names and with slight variations to the recipe.

Serves: 6
Preparation: 30 minutes + 1 hour's chilling
for the pastry
Cooking: 1¼ hours
Recipe grading: fairly easy

For the pastry:

- 1⅔ cups/250 g all-purpose/plain flour
- ½ cup/100 g superfine/caster sugar
- ½ cup/125 g butter, softened
- 1 whole egg and 1 egg yolk
- 1 teaspoon baking powder
- 2 amaretti cookies, crushed
- 1 tablespoon rum

For the custard:

- 1¼ cups/300 ml whole milk
- shaving of lemon zest
- 3 large egg yolks
- 3 tablespoons superfine/caster sugar
- 2 tablespoons all-purpose/plain flour
- ½ teaspoon vanilla extract/essence
- pat/nut of butter

For the filling:

- 10 ladyfingers/sponge fingers
- 15 amaretti cookies, crushed
- 1½ cups/375 ml Alchermes liqueur
- 10 oz/300 g semisweet/dark chocolate, coarsely grated

Torta di amaretti e cioccolato

Amaretti and chocolate cake

Put the flour, sugar, butter, egg and egg yolk, baking powder, crushed amaretti cookies, and rum together in a bowl. Use your fingers to combine these ingredients into a firm dough. ▪ Shape the dough into a ball, then wrap in plastic wrap (cling film) and place in the refrigerator for 1 hour. ▪ Prepare the custard by placing the milk in a saucepan with the lemon zest. Bring to a gentle boil. ▪ In a separate bowl, beat the egg yolks with the sugar, then stir in the flour. ▪ Remove the lemon shaving from the hot milk. Then gradually, adding a little at a time, pour the milk into the egg mixture. ▪ Transfer the mixture to the saucepan and return to a moderate heat until the custard thickens, stirring continuously. ▪ Add the vanilla extract and butter and stir well. Remove the custard from the heat and leave to cool. ▪ Roll out the pastry dough and use half of it to line an 8 in/20 cm diameter springform cake pan. ▪ Cover with a layer of custard followed by a layer of ladyfingers and amaretti cookies (briefly dipped in the Alchermes liqueur), and a layer of chocolate. Repeat the process until all the ingredients have been used up. ▪ Cover with the other half of the pastry dough. ▪ Prick the surface with the prongs of a fork. Bake in a preheated oven at 350°F/180°C/gas 4 for 1 hour. ▪ Serve at room temperature.

Serves: 6
Preparation: 2 hours + 2–3 days' resting for the filling
Cooking: 25 minutes
Recipe grading: complicated

For the filling:
- scant 1 cup/125 g walnuts
- ¾ cup/90 g fine dry bread crumbs
- 1 cup/325 g chunky jam
- 1¾ cups/500 g clear runny honey
- ½ cup/125 ml water
- ½ cup/90 g seedless golden raisins/ sultanas, soaked in water, well drained
- ½ cup/90 g pine nuts
- dash of ground cinnamon

For the pastry:
- 2 cups/300 g all-purpose/plain flour
- ½ cup/100 g superfine/caster sugar
- dash of salt
- finely grated zest of 1 lemon
- ⅔ cup/150 g butter, cut into small pieces
- 1 whole egg and 2 egg yolks
- confectioners'/icing sugar

Spongata

Christmas pie

Chop the walnuts finely. ▪ Spread the bread crumbs out on a shallow baking sheet. Place in a moderate oven to brown lightly. ▪ Chop the fruit pieces in the jam into very small pieces. ▪ Place the jam, walnuts, and bread crumbs in a mixing bowl. ▪ Pour the honey into a small saucepan with the water and bring slowly to a boil. ▪ Stir into the mixing bowl with the nut and bread crumb mixture. Add the golden raisins, pine nuts, and cinnamon. Mix well. ▪ Cover the bowl with a clean cloth and leave to stand in a cool place (not in the refrigerator) for 2–3 days. ▪ To make the pastry, sift the flour into a mixing bowl. Add the sugar, salt, and lemon zest (with no pith) and mix well. ▪ Turn out onto a pastry board and heap up into a mound. Make a well in the center, then add the butter, using your fingertips to rub it into the flour. The mixture should resemble fine crumbs. ▪ Add the egg and egg yolks and combine, working the pastry dough briefly. Shape it into a ball and cover with plastic wrap (cling film). Chill in the refrigerator for 1 hour. ▪ Divide the dough in two portions, one slightly larger than the other. Roll them out into two disks, trimming one to 9½ in/24 cm, the other to 11 in/ 28 cm in diameter. (Use the lower edges of suitable size saucepan lids, dipped in flour, for neatness.) ▪ Place a sheet of silicone baking paper on a baking sheet and transfer the smaller disk carefully onto it. ▪ Give the filling a final stir and spoon it onto the pastry dough, spreading it out, but leaving a ½ in/1 cm border all round the edge. ▪ Cover with the large disk, pressing the border and edges to seal well (trim off any overlapping dough from the larger disk). Bake in a preheated oven at 375°F/190°C/ gas 5 for 25 minutes. ▪ Leave to cool before sprinkling with sifted confectioners' sugar.

A classic Renaissance dessert, usually served at Christmas time. It is a specialty of two Emilian towns, Brescello *and* Busseto, *the latter being the birthplace of Giuseppe Verdi.*

Artusi: the father of Italian cooking

Pellegrino Artusi was born at Forlimpopoli, in Emilia Romagna, in 1820, the son of a grocer. In 1851 the Artusi family moved to Florence, where the young Artusi became a banker. It was not until he was nearly sixty that he began to devote himself to gastronomy. With characteristic punctiliousness, he decided to approach the subject scientifically. Assisted by a young cook and a waiter, he painstakingly tried out recipes over and over again and gradually compiled a cook book. Although *La scienza in cucina e l'arte di mangiare bene* (Science in the Kitchen and the Art of Eating Well) reflected Artusi's own preference for Tuscan and Emilian food, it included recipes from every region of Italy and was a first attempt to capture Italian cooking as a whole. In 1891 Artusi published the book at his own expense and gave it to his friends and acquaintances. Gradually its readership widened and it became a symbol of united Italy, as well as a huge publishing success. English translations of the book are now available.

In the introduction, the author declares his love for "the beautiful and the good, wherever they are to be found." He describes himself as an amateur and therefore easily understood by all those who approach cooking without any particular qualifications or experience. Artusi also states that he is not a very hearty eater and certainly not a glutton: this is difficult to believe, considering the obsessive care with which he collected and tried out the recipes for his book over many years. He goes on to advise against too much reliance on cook books because "they are nearly always unreliable and incomprehensible, especially the Italian ones," and later declares that French recipe books are better, but only when the apprentice cook already has some experience. The author urges his readers, furthermore, to be willing to persevere, citing his own experience as a bachelor and a misanthrope: necessary qualities for a banker-cum-amateur cook who surprised and delighted united Italy with her first book of national cuisine.

Artusi reveals his predilection for Tuscan and Emilian cooking by modifying many of southern Italy's typical dishes, reducing the amount of garlic, onion, spices, and pepper and considerably increasing the use of meat, butter, and sauces, in keeping with the cooking of central and northern Italy. The book was aimed at the bourgeoisie, the rising class of the time, whose members longed to display their newly acquired wealth and could afford to buy the products recommended by Artusi (notably meat which was very expensive in those days.)

Artusi's Fruit Tarts

Although Artusi claimed that he was not a glutton, he was apparently very fond of fruit-covered tarts for dessert. This recipe for sweet plain pastry was the one he recommended to use for the base in these tarts.

1¾ cups/275 g all-purpose/plain flour
¾ cup/125 g confectioners'/icing sugar
scant ½ cup/100 g butter, softened
4 tablespoons lard, softened
4 large egg yolks
1 teaspoon finely grated orange zest/rind (optional)
1 cup/300 g jam (raspberry, strawberry, or plum)

Combine the flour and confectioners' sugar in a bowl and add the butter, lard, egg yolks, and orange zest, if using. Working quickly (pastry should be kneaded as little as possible, to keep it light), use your fingertips to combine. When the ingredients are thoroughly combined, shape into a ball and wrap in plastic wrap (cling film). Set aside to rest for at least 30 minutes. Divide the dough into two parts, one of which is twice as large as the other. Use a rolling pin to shape the larger piece into a round and use it to line the buttered and floured bottom and sides of a shallow baking pan. Prick the pastry with the prongs of a fork. Spread evenly with the jam. Roll the remaining pastry out and cut into strips. Decorate the top of the tart with these in a lattice shape. Bake in a preheated oven at 350°F/180°C/gas 4 for about 30 minutes. Serve hot or at room temperature.

The beauty of Artusi's writing is that he does not confine himself to recipes but embellishes them with anecdotes, asides about customs, historical details, dietetic observations, and helpful advice for young mothers and housewives. Pellegrino Artusi was certainly the first Italian to understand the importance of a culinary tradition within the family—the note books with their scrawled recipes for dishes linked with special memories ("the cook's recipe for the croquettes we had at the Ribolinis' at Easter," and the like).

Serves: 6
Preparation: 40 minutes
Cooking: 15 minutes
Recipe grading: easy

- 2 cups/300 g very fine yellow cornmeal
- 1⅓ cups/200 g all-purpose/plain flour
- ½ cup/100 g superfine/caster sugar
- dash of salt
- finely grated zest of 1 lemon
- ⅔ cup/150 g butter, cut into small pieces
- 4 tablespoons milk
- generous ½ cup/100 g seedless golden raisins/sultanas, soaked in water, then drained and squeezed of excess moisture
- ⅓ cup/60 g pine nuts
- confectioners'/icing sugar

Suggested wine: a sweet white
(Albana Dolce)

Zalett

Cornmeal, pine nut, and raisin cookies

Sift the cornmeal and flour into a mixing bowl. Combine with the sugar, salt, and lemon zest (without any of the white pith). ▪ Turn out onto a pastry board and heap up into a mound. Make a well in the center and add the butter and the milk. ▪ Gradually combine these ingredients with the flour, adding a little more milk if necessary. The dough should be firm. ▪ Work the dough, incorporating the seedless golden raisins and pine nuts. ▪ Break off pieces of dough about the size of a large walnut. Shape them into balls, then flatten slightly. ▪ Place them, well spaced out, on greased and floured baking sheet(s). ▪ Bake in a preheated oven at 400°F/200°C/gas 6 for 15 minutes. ▪ Cool on a rack. Dust with the confectioners' sugar and serve.

These delicious little cornmeal cookies are made to an old Romagnol recipe. Mix a few drops of vanilla extract (essence) with the milk.

Torta di riso

Rice cake

Bring the milk to a boil in a heavy-bottomed saucepan with the salt. ▪ Add the rice and simmer over a low heat, stirring very frequently, until it is done. ▪ Remove from the heat, then stir in the sugar, followed by the lemon zest (without any of the white pith). Leave to cool to room temperature. ▪ Stir in the almonds, almond extract, and egg yolks. ▪ Beat the egg whites with a dash of salt until very firm and fold into the rice mixture, using a metal spoon so as not to crush the air out of the egg whites. ▪ Grease a 9½ in/24 cm cake pan with butter, then sprinkle with bread crumbs. Spoon the mixture into it. ▪ Bake in a preheated oven at 350°F/180°C/gas 4 for 40 minutes.

Serves: 6
Preparation: 45 minutes + cooling
Cooking: 1 hour
Recipe grading: fairly easy

- 4½ cups/1 liter milk
- dash of salt
- 1¼ cups/250 g Arborio or pudding rice
- scant ½ cup/90 g superfine/caster sugar
- finely grated zest of 1 lemon
- 1 cup/100 g finely chopped toasted almonds
- 2–3 drops almond extract/essence
- 4 large eggs, separated
- dash of salt

Suggested wine: a sweet white
(Colli Piacentini Malvasia Dolce)

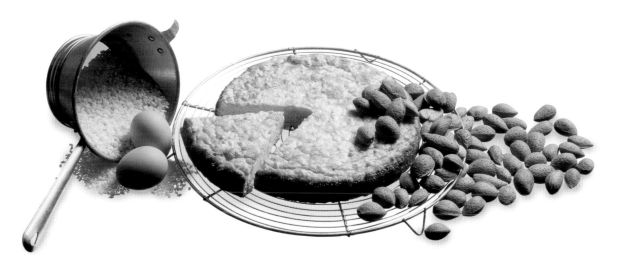

Nowadays this Emilian cake is also made with a thin, sweet pastry case, but the above recipe is the most traditional.

Torta nera

Black pie

Mix the sifted flour, salt, sugar, and baking powder together in a bowl. ▪ Turn out onto a pastry board and heap up into a mound. Make a well in the center and add the butter. ▪ Rub the butter into the dry ingredients with your fingertips. The resulting mixture will look like fine bread crumbs. ▪ Add the egg yolks and liqueur or rum and combine. Work briefly to form a smooth dough. ▪ Mix the almonds in a bowl with the sugar and sifted cocoa powder. ▪ Stir in the egg yolks and coffee, blending well. ▪ Roll out the pastry and line a fairly shallow 10 in/25 cm springform pie or cake pan previously greased with butter and dusted with flour. ▪ Pinch all round the edge of the pastry to obtain a fluted effect. ▪ Fill the pie shell with the filling. Do not smooth the surface level. ▪ Bake in a preheated oven at 350°F/180°C/gas 4 for 35 minutes. ▪ Serve warm.

Serves: 4–6
Preparation: 45 minutes
Cooking: 45 minutes
Recipe grading: fairly easy

- 1⅔ cups/250 g all-purpose/plain flour
- dash of salt
- ⅓ cup/70 g superfine/caster sugar
- 2 teaspoons baking powder
- ½ cup/125 g butter, cut in small pieces
- 2 large egg yolks
- 2 tablespoons Sassolino liqueur or Jamaica rum

For the filling:
- 1½ cups/150 g finely chopped toasted almonds
- ¾ cup/150 g superfine/caster sugar
- ½ cup/75 g unsweetened cocoa powder
- 2 large egg yolks
- 5 tablespoons strong coffee, cooled

Suggested wine: a dry sparkling white (Colli Piacentini Malvasia Spumante Secco)

This recipe comes from San Secondo, in the province of Parma. The sweet pastry breaks very easily, so be sure to handle it carefully when you take it out of the pan to serve.

Budino di riso dell'Artusi

Rice pudding Artusi-style

Serves: 8
Preparation: 15 minutes
Cooking: 35 minutes
Recipe grading: easy

- ¾ cup/150 g Arborio or pudding rice
- 4¼ cups/1 liter milk
- 1 vanilla bean/pod
- scant ½ cup/90 g superfine/caster sugar
- ½ cup/90 g golden raisins/sultanas
- 1½ tablespoons chopped candied peel
- dash of salt
- pat/nut of butter
- 2 whole eggs and 2 egg yolks
- 1 cup/250 ml rum or cognac
- 4 tablespoons bread crumbs

Suggested wine: a sparkling dry or medium white (Bianco di Scandiano Spumante Secco, Brut, or Amabile)

Bring the rice, milk, and vanilla bean to a boil and simmer for 10 minutes. ▪ Add the sugar, raisins, peel, salt, and butter. When cooked, remove from the heat and leave to cool. ▪ Add the eggs and egg yolks and then the rum. Pour this mixture into the pudding basin which has been coated with the bread crumbs. ▪ Bake in a preheated oven at 180°C/350°F/gas 4 for about 35 minutes. ▪ Unmold and serve while still warm.

Pellegrino Artusi's classic book (see pages 110–111), was the first book of national cuisine to be published after Italy was united. Over one hundred years later, it is still the best-selling cook book in Italy today. Here is one of his classic desserts.

A

Adriatic seafood soup 62
Amaretti and chocolate cake 106
Anguilla all'uso di Comacchio 83
Arista alla reggiana 64
Artusi, Pellegrino 110–111
Asparagi alla parmigiana 98
Asparagus with parmesan cheese 98

B

Baked lasagna Bologna-style 38
Balsamic vinegar 92–93
Bensone 103
Black pie 115
Bolognese cutlets 61
Bomba di riso alla piacentina 49
Braised red mullet 87
Brandy-flavored fritters 105
Brodetto dell'adriatico 62
Budino di riso dell'Artusi 116

C

Calf's liver with balsamic vinegar 71
Canocchie ripiene 86
Cappellacci di zucca 36
Cappelletti di magro romagnoli 33
Cappone ripieno 73
Cassoni 16
Cheese and potato pie 94
Cheese dumpling soup 37
Chilled layered veal and ham mold 74
Christmas pie 108
Clam soup 52
Cornmeal, pine nut, and raisin cookies 112

Cotechino in galera 82
Cotechino sausage with beef and vegetables 82
Cotolette alla bolognese 61
Cotolette alla parmigiana 65
Crescenti 18
Cristoforo Messisbugo and the dukes of Este in Ferrara 76–77

E

Eel risotto 58
Emilian trifle 101
Endive with pancetta and balsamic vinegar 89
Erbazzone 24

F

Fegato all'aceto balsamico 71
Flatbreads 15, 22–23
Fresh pasta 46–47
Fried eggy bread with cheese and prosciutto 81
Fried mortadella 19
Fried pumpkin 96
Fried vegetable pies 16
Frittatine all'aceto balsamico 31
Fritters in balsamic vinegar 31
Fritto alla garisenda 81
Frizon 99

G

Garganelli con ragù and pisellini 44
Gelato di parmigiano 27

H

Hunter's chicken 70

I

Insalata all'aceto balsamico 26

J

Jam-filled turnovers 104

L

Lasagne alla bolognese 38

M

Macaroni pie Ferrara-style 56
Malmaritati 43
Marinated eggplants 95
Meat sauce 40
Melanzane marinate 95
Modena cake 103
Mortadella fritta 19

P

Parma ham 84–85
Parmesan cheese 40–41
Parmesan cheese ice cream 27
Passatelli 37
Pasta and bean soup 43
Pasta ripiena alla brisighellese 48
Pasta with meat sauce and peas 44
Pasticcio alla ferrarese 56
Piadina 15
Pollo alla cacciatora 70
Potato pie 29
Prosciutto con melone 30
Prosciutto from Parma 84–85
Prosciutto with melon 30

R

Radicchio all'aceto balsamico 89

Ribbon noodles with prosciutto 55

Rice and pumpkin pie 20

Rice cake 113

Rice Piacenza-style 49

Rice pudding Artusi-style 116

Rifreddo 74

Risotto all'anguilla 58

Risotto col pesce san pietro 59

Risotto with John Dory 59

Roast pork Reggio-style 64

Roast stuffed capon 73

Romagnol stuffed pasta 33

Rossal 87

Rotolo ripieno 50

S

Salad with balsamic vinegar dressing 26

Savory onions and tomatoes 99

Savory pastry fritters 18

Savory pie 24

Sfrappole 105

Spongata 108

Stewed eel Comacchio-style 83

Stuffed pasta with cheese filling 48

Stuffed broiled shrimp 86

Stuffed pasta roll 50

Stuffed pasta with pumpkin filling 36

Stuffed pasta with spinach and ricotta filling 53

Stuffed pig's trotter with lentils 79

Stuffed zucchini 90

T

Tagliatelle al prosciutto 55

Torta di amaretti e cioccolato 106

Torta di patate 29

Torta di riso 113

Torta di riso con la zucca 20

Torta nera 115

Tortelli alle erbette 53

Tortelli di marmellata 104

Tortellini in brodo 35

Tortellini in meat stock 35

Tortino di patate 94

V

Valigini 67

Veal cutlets Parma-style 65

Veal rolls 67

W

Wines of Emilia Romagna 68–69

Z

Zalett 112

Zampone con lenticchie 79

Zucca fritta 96

Zucchine ripiene 90

Zuppa all'emiliana 101

Zuppa di poveracce 52

Acknowledgments

The Publishers would like to thank Mastrociliegia, Fiesole (Florence) who kindly lent props for photography.

All photos by Marco Lanza except:

Farabolafoto, Milan: 1, 2, 5, 6, 8, 9, 11t, 12 t, 13, 22t, 23, 41br, 47, 68l, 69, 84b, 85, 93tl;
Giuseppe Carfagna, Rome: 7b, 12b, 20t, 68r, 93br Adriano Nardi, Florence: 3, 11b;
Archivio Scala, Florence: 76; Overseas, Milan 41bl, 41t, 84t;
Illustrations: Ivan Stalio 92t, 93c, 93tr; Paola Ravaglia: 7